The Shape of Participation

The Shape of Participation

A Theology of Church Practices

L. ROGER OWENS

CASCADE *Books* · Eugene, Oregon

THE SHAPE OF PARTICIPATION
A Theology of Church Practices

Cascade Books
An Imprint of Wipf and Stock Publishers
199 W. 8th Ave., Suite 3
Eugene, OR 97401

www.wipfandstock.com

ISBN 13: 978-1-60608-519-6

Cataloging-in-Publication data:

Owens, L. Roger.

The shape of participation : a theology of church practices / L. Roger Owens.

x + 198 p. ; 23 cm. — Includes bibliographical references and index.

ISBN 13: 978-1-60608-519-6

1. Theology, Practical. 2. Christian communties. 3. Church—History of
Doctrines. 4. Bonhoeffer, Dietrich, 1906–1945. 5. McCabe, Herbert, 1926– .
6. MacIntyre, Alasdair C. I. Title.

BV3 .094 2010

For Ginger

Contents

Preface

M Y WRITING ON CHURCH practices began at Duke University, first as a Duke Divinity student and later as a PhD student in the graduate program in religion. While many there encouraged me along the way, I want to offer a special word of thanks to the faculty on my dissertation committee. My advisor, Stanley Hauerwas, has been more than an advisor. We have been members of the same church, where he often sat in the front pew while I preached. Seven years ago I sat on the front row while he preached at my wedding. His honesty as a parishioner, his truthfulness as a preacher, and his availability, prodding, and good cheer as an advisor have made what for many is a process of drudgery, for me pure joy (mingled, of course, with some drudgery). I also want to thank L. Gregory Jones, Reinhard Hütter, Richard Lischer, and J. Carter for their encouragement, availability, and insight.

Without the friendship of Beth and Brian Felker Jones I could not have found my way to the end of this project. Our conversations, often over cheap Chinese food, helped me find my way both in the world of theology and in life. Traci Smith has been a wonderful, supportive friend as well. Traci's desire to be a faithful witness has always inspired me to greater faithfulness.

Not many working on a PhD have had the good fortune to have a brother like mine who had already finished his. The hurdles and pitfalls were fresh enough in Bo's memory that he was an invaluable guide through the process. More importantly, he is a model human being in his commitment to living decently and well. I count our relationship as one of God's greatest gifts in my life. Another of those great gifts is the gift of two wonderful parents, Max and Gayle Owens. I hope I am as loving and generous toward my own children as they have been toward me.

Those children, Simeon Nathaniel, Silas Zachariah, and, now, Mary Clare—anything I could say about the joy they bring to my life would be mere clichés. The only thing I have hated about writing this book is the time it has kept me from spending with them. Finally, I thank Ginger, but I cannot list the things I thank her for. She is my partner in life and in the gospel. Any list would only minimize how completely I thank her and love her. In this world I have no greater friend, no greater love, and no greater gift.

Introduction: Practicing Communities

E VERY WEEK AS PASTORS my wife and I lead a medium sized, urban
United Methodist congregation in a number of practices. We worship
together. We hear the Scriptures read and proclaimed. We celebrate the
Lord's Supper. We welcome the guests in our midst. Outside of Sunday
morning we do a good deal of eating together. We pray and study Scripture
together. We participate in what John Wesley called the "means of grace"
and what theologians and practitioners are increasingly describing as
Christian practices. These practices make us who we are. They constitute
our life together.

As a theologian, I reflect on these practices. What is it about these
practices that makes us "church" and not some other voluntary associa-
tion? How do these activities, these practices, relate to what God is doing
in the world? How do they open us to the life of God and open the world
to the life of God? How do the several practices that make up the life of
a congregation—hospitality, singing, keeping Sabbath, offering testimony—relate to the liturgically central and constitutive practices of baptism,
preaching, and the Eucharist?

When I think about the future of mainline Protestantism in North
America, and especially my own United Methodist Church, about how we
will face the quickly changing and increasingly complex new century we
have just begun, I am convinced that these questions are crucial in order
for the church to understand its identity and mission. These church practices need to be grounded theologically in order to reinvigorate ecclesiology and mission. A movement to understand congregations as made up of
a web of central, vital practices is turning around mainline congregations
and giving them new life. The helpful literature on Christian practices
continues to proliferate. But this movement requires serious theological
articulation to make sure it is oriented toward faithfulness to the triune
God who calls us to these practices and not toward a pragmatic concern
for the survival of religious institutions.

My purpose in writing this book is to offer just such a theological account, an account rich enough to support the ever expanding use of the language of church practices as those very practices continue to help churches experience new life. I present a theology of Christian practices rooted in the life of the triune God in order to orient the church toward faithfulness to this very God. The heartbeat of this book is the conviction that church practices *are* the church's participation in God's own life through the union of our bodies with God's. And that means participation in God is embodied. It is visible. Participation has a particular shape.

WHOSE CHURCH? WHICH PRACTICES?

Whose Church?

Before I go on, I want to be clear about two things. When I talk about church practices, whose church and which practices am I talking about? That the church today is divided, divided both between East and West and Roman Catholic and Protestant, is the greatest impediment to the church's proclaiming the gospel with integrity. This division is also the greatest impediment to doing theology, because, like it or not, the theologian inhabits a divided ecclesial space. How handy it would be if we who write about the church could abstract ourselves from our particularities and overcome our division with the mind. But this book is about how the church in its embodied particularity participates in the life of God, and that embodied particularity is inescapably broken. To deny the fact or ignore it is to write about a church that does not exist.

I wish I had an answer to how to practice church and do theology with integrity out of a church that bears the wounds of division, but I don't. On the other hand, I don't think such a situation should stop us from doing our best to continue to think about what it means to be the church that shares in the life of God. As Robert Jenson argues, continuing to practice theology for *the* church, and refusing to do theology for *a* church, is part of the church's patience as the church waits to apprehend the fullness of her being "only in the coming Kingdom."[1] While acknowledging the wound of a broken, divided church, I write about church practices. I know that I inhabit shaky ecclesial territory—we all do—but I know no where else to stand.

---

1. Jenson, *Triune God*, viii.

On the other hand, I cannot escape my own ecclesial territory. I am a United Methodist pastor and theologian. But this book is not United Methodist theology. Indeed, I don't know what that would look like. What is peculiarly Methodist about this book, however, is my willingness to draw from a variety of theological resources across the Christian landscape. John Wesley himself was willing to learn from whomever was helpful—whether the Eastern Fathers or Moravian missionaries. As a theologian and pastor in a church that never intended to be a church, I carry on the tradition of drawing from across the Christian traditions—so the German Lutheran Dietrich Bonhoeffer helps me think through a theology of preaching, while the Dominican Herbert McCabe helps me think through a theology of the Lord's Supper. Maximus the Confessor shows up near the end to help me pull the various strands of the argument together. And for this I do not apologize nor do I offer a theory of the church that legitimates such eclecticism.

Though this is not United Methodist theology—I hope it is *Christian* theology—my deep concern is for my own denomination and for others like it, namely, mainline denominations in North America struggling to understand what it means for them to be church when their social influence has waned. These churches still have a divine calling and destiny; they still have a divine constitution; and they still have a divine mission. In this work of Christian theology, I aim to help other pastors like me and other churches like mine understand what we do and what we should do as we practice our faith through the corporate practices that make us who we are. As theologian Sam Wells has said about his recent book on Christian ethics, so I say about this book in ecclesiology: "This is not a paper debate: it is a call for the renewal of the Church."[2]

Which Practices?

What are those corporate practices that make us who we are? What is the difference between Christian practices in general and church-constitutive practices? A great deal of excellent literature has been written on Christian practices, and the practices enumerated continue to proliferate. Here are some examples: honoring the body, hospitality, household economics, saying yes and saying no, keeping sabbath, giving testimony, discerning, shaping communities, forgiving, healing, dying well, singing

2. Wells, *God's Companions*, 2.

our lives, praying, iconography, celebrating the Lord's Supper, fellow-shipping at table, serving, education, baptism, contemplation, theology, liturgy, and Scripture interpretation.[3] This list ranges from what might be called core or constitutive practices—Lord's Supper and baptism, for instance—to practices more difficult to define and relate to the identity of the church—like saying yes and saying no, for instance. As the literature on Christian practices continues to grow, thinking about the relationship between core or constitutive practices, those practices without which the church would not be the church, and peripheral but important practices, those practices key to helping disciples and churches embody their call-ing in different ways, is ever more important.

The theology of church practices I offer in this book revolves around a discussion of two constitutive practices—preaching and Eucharist. These are the practices that most regularly ground the week-to-week life of most congregations. The standard liturgy in my own denomination is the liturgy of Word and Table. The movement from the reading and proclamation of Scripture to the Lord's Supper shapes our weekly wor-ship and the pattern of our life together. However one enumerates the list of Christian practices, a theology of Christian practices should emerge from a consideration of the shape of constitutive church practices. While they are not the only constitutive practices, the two practices of preaching and Eucharist are just such core, constitutive practices. The argument of this book does not rest on establishing a definitive list of either Christian practices or church-constitutive practices. Rather, it rests on the assump-tion that beginning with what I consider to be undeniably constitutive practices, easily recognizable to the vast majority of Christian congrega-tions, will lay the foundation to explore a theology of other practices—like keeping sabbath and honoring the body—practices that, while important, are not strictly church-constitutive.

PRACTICING COMMUNITIES

In a theological study of embodied church practices as participation in the life of God, it will do no good to discuss practices merely theoretically or in the abstract. Since the practices I am writing about are embodied and corporate, I must be able to point to particular communities that ex-

3. This list comes from three sources: Bass, *Practicing Our Faith*; Weaver-Zercher and Willimon, *Vital Christianity*; and Buckley and Yeago, *Knowing the Triune God*.

emplify these practices. More importantly, the central questions I address in this book—questions about how church practices relate to God's activity, how they make up the church's embodied life, and how they relate the world to God's re-creative purposes—*arise* out of a consideration of the lives of real communities. Thus I begin this book with a description of the lives of two Christian communities and their own self-understandings to show how the practices of these communities point in the direction of a theology of church practices as embodied participation in God. Furthermore, since this book focuses on the practices of preaching and Eucharist, I've chosen two communities for which these practices are especially central. The practices of early Methodist societies and classes and the worshipping life of Mt. Level Missionary Baptist Church begin to show how Christian communities, as they practice their corporate lives in the world, embody for the world the very life of God.

Sharing God's Life in Early Methodist Practice

In this autobiographical account of his conversion, John Barritt describes the shape of early Methodist practice:

> ...1773, when I was about 17 years of age I providentially heard a Methodist preacher, namely Mr. Bardsly. His text was Isaiah 3:10.
> ...
>
> I went home weeping and continued to weep and pray for near a month. ... I went to hear again and the preacher was Mr. Thomas Taylor. He preached from the evidence given to Job by his friends. ... In his discourse he told us that all by nature were unacquainted with God and had no true peace. He proceeded to preach to us how we might become acquainted with the Lord so as to find pardon and peace.
>
> I was much enlightened by his discourse and joined the society, and the first time I met in class my knowledge of the plan of salvation through Jesus Christ was much increased. I prayed at all opportunities, in the house, barn, and fields; and I soon found peace with God ...
>
> 1774 Then I went on my way rejoicing. Perhaps a year after this we had Mr. William Brammah on our circuit. He frequently preached on the subject of sanctification; and by hearing him I began to understand that it was my privilege to advance in the divine life, and I got Mr. Wesley's thoughts on *Christian Perfection* and read it carefully over. ... I recollected we prayed to the Almighty at church to cleanse the thoughts of our hearts by the inspira-

tion of his Spirit and I began to think that these words and similar expressions must mean something. . . . On sabbath days I went to Padiham and heard Mr. Brammah preach from these words . . . and I found the Lord speak to my heart . . . and I found a glorious change and my soul was filled with love to God and man.[4]

Tom Albin, who has studied hundreds of such autobiographical accounts, concludes that "the pattern represented in John Barrit's diary is more the norm than the exception."[5] This description points to three important aspects of the shape of early Methodist practice: the role of preaching; the role of participation in societies and classes; and the emphasis on sanctification as a process of growing in "the divine life."

THE ROLE OF PREACHING IN EARLY METHODISM

John Barrit's account of his own conversion does not confirm the stereotypical understanding of revival preaching in which a sudden change of heart is rendered in the hearer after the sermon. His account shows the much more usual pattern in which the preaching, either in the open air or in the societies, existed in relationship to and nourished the life of the societies and classes. Preaching was one focus of a dual foci revival, the goal of which was, as Theodore Runyan says, the "renewal of the creation and the creatures through the renewal in humanity of the *image of God.* . . ."[6] The Methodists called this renewal sanctification, growing in divine life. As Barritt's account makes clear, the practice of preaching was an ongoing part of this process of renewal and an integral aspect of the life of early Methodism.

PARTICIPATION IN SOCIETIES AND CLASSES

Barritt's account points to the societies and classes as the heart of the shape of early Methodist practice. The purpose of these societies and their weekly class meetings was to offer members accountable discipleship, a disciplined setting in which they could share with one another the shape of their own lives of discipleship.[7] The shape of the discussion was established by the General Rules as historian David Lowes Watson describes them:

4. Quoted in Albin, "Empirical Study," 275–76.

5. Ibid., 279.

6. Runyan, *New Creation*, 8.

7. Watson, *Early Methodist Class Meeting*, 90–91.

> The *Rules* accordingly stipulated three criteria. First, members
> were enjoined to do no harm, and to avoid "evil in every kind."
> Second, they were to do good "of every possible sort, and as far
> as possible, to all Men." Third, they were to attend upon "all the
> Ordinances of God; Such are The publick Worship of God; the
> Ministry of the Word, either read or expounded; The Supper of
> the Lord; Private Prayer; Searching the Scriptures; and Fasting, or
> Abstinence." Wesley regarded this third criterion, the attending on
> the ordinances of God, as availing oneself of the "instituted means
> of grace," the disciplines, the practices of the church, without which
> any attempt to pursue a Christian discipleship was fallacious.[8]

As the third rule shows, the class meetings did not exist as ends in
themselves, but to support and encourage the member's participation
in the practices and disciplines that constitute the church and the life of
discipleship.

For Wesley, chief among these practices was the public worship of
God and the sacrament of the Lord's Supper. In fact, the Methodist revival
was as much a sacramental revival as it was an evangelical revival. The
Eucharistic celebration was a crucial part of the Methodist evangelical
revival.[9] The Eucharist was central not only to the practice of John and
Charles Wesley but also in the practices of the societies. As early as the
1740s the societies in Bristol and London were having Eucharistic cel-
ebrations in their own meeting houses weekly—a much more frequent
celebration than in the Church of England parishes at the time. "There
can be no doubt that, with only rare exceptions, the Methodist people
dearly prized the Lord's Supper."[10] Participation in the Lord's Supper was
one of the practices that gave early Methodism its distinctive shape.

Like an ellipse around two foci, the practices of Methodist communities, including the structures of the itinerant ministry and the shape
of the societies, classes, and bands, revolved around preaching and the
celebration of the Lord's Supper. The other practices were related to these
two central practices and took their intelligibility from them. Preaching
often led people into the societies and classes, as Barritt's autobiography
indicates. Preaching also nourished and challenged them while in the
classes. The classes themselves functioned to support the members in

8. Ibid., 108.

9. Bowmer, *Sacrament*, 187–209.

10. Ibid., 193.

embodying the shape of Christ's own life in the world. That embodiment involved attending to particular practices, especially participation in the Lord's Supper.

SANCTIFICATION AS PARTICIPATION IN THE DIVINE LIFE

Is there a theological rational that makes sense of these practices and gives the movement in general some intelligibility? The third point from Barritt's spiritual autobiography gestures toward just such a rationale: the goal of sanctification, of growing in "the divine life." The writings of both John and Charles Wesley reveal that participation in the life of God is central for understanding the practices of early Methodist communities. References to 2 Peter 1:4 in the work of John and "participation" language in the hymns of Charles show that they understood sanctification to be growth in participation in the divine life.

In John Wesley's *A Farther Appeal to Men of Reason and Religion* (1745), one of the early tracts defending Methodism, John articulates his understanding of salvation with an important allusion to participation in God. He writes,

> By salvation I mean, not barely (according to the vulgar notion) deliverance from hell, or going to heaven, but a present deliverance from sin, a restoration of the soul to its primitive health, its original purity; a recovery of the divine nature; the renewal of our souls after the image of God in righteousness and true holiness, in justice, mercy, and truth. This implies all holy and heavenly tempers, and by consequence all holiness in conversation.[11]

For Wesley, salvation as holiness is a *recovery of the divine nature*, which he equates with a restoration in the human being of the image of God. These two concepts are closely linked for Wesley. In his *Explanatory Notes upon the New Testament*, he comments on 2 Peter 1:4, saying that partaking of the divine nature is "being renewed in the image of God, and having communion with him, so as to dwell in God, and God in you."[12] For Wesley the restoration of the image of God through Christ just is participation in the divine nature; and since this is also salvation as holiness,

---

11. Wesley, "Farther Appeal," 106.
12. Quoted in Long, *Wesley's Moral Theology*, 198.

it is clear that for Wesley participation in God is shown in the shape of the Christian's life. It is visible.[13]

Charles, too, made use of this language especially in his hymns.[14] In one hymn on the incarnation, Charles writes, "He deigns in flesh to appear, / Widest extremes to join; / To bring our vileness near, / And make us all divine.... Then shall his love be fully showed, / And man shall then be lost in God."[15] Here Charles takes up the early Christian theme that Christ became a human so humans might become divine. Similar language appears in a hymn to the Holy Spirit: "Eager for thee I ask and pant; / So strong, the principle divine / Carries me out, with sweet constraint, / Till all my hallowed soul is thine; / Plunged in the Godhead's deepest sea, And lost in thine immensity."[16] Again, the language of deification occurs in the following lines: "Heavenly Adam, Life divine / Change my nature into thine; / Move and spread throughout my soul, / Actuate and fill the whole; / Be it I no longer now / Living in the flesh, but thou."[17] In these lines Charles uses the language of deification to link participation in God with life in the flesh, so that participation in God is not an escape from our materiality but is, rather, God's enfleshing our own flesh, so to speak, in a way appropriate to our created natures.

But how, and where, does God's enfleshing of us happen? For Charles, it happens supremely in the Eucharist. He writes in a eucharistic hymn, "Saviour, Thou didst this Mystery give, / That I Thy nature might partake; Thou biddest me outward signs receive, / One with Thyself my soul to make; / My body, soul, and spirit join / Inseparably one with Thine." According to Charles, union with God occurs in the celebration of the Eucharist. As with John, the union Charles describes is not that of an invisible essence united mystically to God. It is the union of the whole person in his materiality transformed into a life of holiness: "My body, soul, and spirit join / Inseparably one with Thine."[18]

I have only sketched an important theme in the work of the Wesleys, a theme that rests at the very heart of their understanding of Christianity

13. See Long, *Wesley's Moral Theology*, 196–201 and Runyan, *New Creation*, 80–81.
14. Allchin, *Participation*, 24–35.
15. Quoted in ibid., 27.
16. Quoted in ibid., 28.
17. Quoted in ibid., 33.
18. Quoted in Bowmer, *Lord's Supper*, 175.

and the Christian life: the Christian life is a life of visible holiness. For the Wesleys, that very holiness is nothing other that participation in the life of God. In our flesh, in our materiality, we partake of the divine nature. The acquisition of holiness, the restoration of the image of God, the recovery of the divine nature—all of these occur in the sociality that is the church. Salvation—participation in the divine—happens in the corporate practices of worship, preaching, prayer, mutual accountability, and the Lord's Supper, practices that are visible in their social embodiment.

This picture of early Methodist practice and its basis in the Wesleys' understanding of participation raises many of the questions I want to address in this book: What does it mean to say the church participates in God? How can this participation be understood in terms of the church's core practices? How is this participation visible? How does this participation make these communities different from other social bodies? These questions push beyond Wesley's own understanding of participation, but they require answers in order to make theological sense of the visible practices of the church and their relationship to the life of the God who is Father, Son, and Holy Spirit

Preaching and Participation at Mt. Level Missionary Baptist Church

On May 1, 2005, Mt. Level Missionary Baptist Church in Durham, North Carolina, celebrated its 141st anniversary. A guest preacher, Dr. James Ballard, preached on the call of Moses in Exodus 3. One did not need to be present in the service of worship very long to know that proclamation did not begin when Dr. Ballard stepped behind the pulpit. Rather, the whole body gathered in worship proclaimed the gospel to itself throughout the service, so that the preacher's sermon was the climax of what had already been going on. This service of worship, from the beginning songs of praise to the Holy Communion in which the pastor "preached" the communion liturgy, shows that Mt. Level's communal identity is shaped by an understanding of itself as a body proclaiming the gospel in its worship and its life.

The service began with the chorus: "In the name of Jesus, we have the victory." This chorus was repeated while the worshipers sang, clapped, and swayed to the rhythm of the piano and the organ. Then, with the piano and the organ still playing, the worship leader stepped into the pulpit and repeated the words of the chorus: "In the name of Jesus, we have the victory." But then his *repetition* of the chorus moved to *conversation* when he asked, "Does anyone have the victory this morning?" That kind of questioning is a common rhetorical strategy in African-American preaching, but here we find the question not on the lips of the preacher, but the worship leader. The congregation responded in the affirmative with handclapping and shouts of, "Amen!" This service of worship began with the proclamation of the gospel in the words of a song and on the lips of the worship leader, a proclamation that turned into a conversation. This style of question and response characterized the whole service and points to the corporate nature of proclamation. Dietrich Bonhoeffer says that in the preaching of the church, church preaches to church (see chapter 3). This "church preaching to church" is evident from the opening minutes of worship at Mt. Level.

After the morning prayer by an elderly lay woman in the congregation, the choir sang its first anthem: "Lift your head, oh ye gates and the King of glory will come in" (Psalm 24) and "God inhabits the praise of his people" (Psalm 22). Following the song the worship leader reiterated the latter affirmation: "Who is the Lord of glory? Do you know who the Lord of glory is? Do you know who he is? He inhabits our praise; he is strong and mighty. I don't know about you, but I need to know that the Lord is strong—he's not lost a battle yet!" This song and the words of the worship leader continued the conversation begun at the beginning of the service, only this time the leader was proclaiming a text from the Psalm in the midst of the life of the congregation. The conversation became a *scriptural* conversation.

The choral anthem also made an important theological affirmation: God's habitation, God's dwelling, is this very activity of praise and proclamation in which the congregation engages. The choral anthem before the sermon reiterated and extended the same theme:

> This is your house, Father, come and dwell, your holy house of prayer.
> We dedicate this temple to you, Lord.
> Be enthroned on the praise of your people.
> Let your glory fill this sanctuary.
> Lord, we agree in unity:
> This is your house, Father, come and dwell, a holy house of prayer.
> Holy Spirit, overflow this place.
> Decorate our walls with grace and mercy.

Let healing and redemption find searching souls.
Lord have your way we humbly pray.
This is your house. . . .

The words of the anthem elaborate on the theme that "God inhabits the praise of his people" by calling the worshiping community itself a sanctuary. Is "house" in the first line the church building or the people who are the temple themselves? The third line suggests the answer: the congregation at praise is the house, the temple, and the throne of the Lord, the very dwelling of God, decorated with the mercy and grace of the Spirit.

The shape of Mt. Level's worship and the theological affirmations made in worship suggest two things. First, the community at praise, a community in conversation with itself and with God, is a community practicing proclamation throughout its service with its whole body. While the words of the preacher are the climax of this practice, the preacher's own preaching extends the conversation that has characterized the whole worship service. Second, the community itself in its activity of praise and proclamation is the dwelling place of God. This theme is not worked out in a systematic way, but is present in the first-order language of worship— the community at praise is the presence of God.

In the same way that the early Methodist communities had the Wesleys to give theological narration to their first-order practice, so Mt. Level has such a theological narrator in their pastor, William C. Turner Jr. Turner, a professor of the practice of homiletics at Duke Divinity School, has in his unpublished sermons[19] and in his book *Discipleship for African American Christians: A Journey through the Church Covenant*[20] given a theological account of the church as the dwelling place of God in a way that highlights the central issues I address in this book.

One sermon in particular raises the theme of participation in an important way.[21] In this sermon Turner preaches about what John Wesley called sanctification, the believer's being renewed in the image of Christ, conformed to the image of the Son. While Wesley associated such conformity with the claim of 2 Peter 1:4 that Christians are "partakers of the divine nature," Turner explores the subject using a different participation

19. Turner, "Preaching the Spirit."
20. Turner, *Discipleship*.
21. Turner, "Conformed to the Image of the Son," in "Preaching the Spirit," 115–22.

motif, one that expresses how our conformity to God's Son is achieved in the body through the work of the Spirit. He writes:

> We are conformed into the image of Christ. We are like icons: through our frame, in our body his beauty shines. We are sort of like the stained window: you don't know how beautiful it is till it gets dark around here, and the light shines through it. Every stain, every line, every impression contributes to the awesome spectacle when the light bursts through. Our features, talents, and gifts are present as an offering. Only by the light of the Spirit do we radiate. Our suffering, our sacrifice, our labor, our obedience—which is nothing of itself—conform us to the image of Christ when the Spirit irradiates us.[22]

Here Turner's language mirrors some of the themes expressed in the worship service, especially in its use of the building to display the congregation's own embodied participation in the light of God. Turner's description of the church as an icon draws special attention to the materiality of participation, for an icon participates in God's glory, becoming a window into God's life. When this understanding of the church as icon is connected to the earlier first-order description of the worshipping community as the dwelling place of God, decorated (or, as here, "beautified") by the Spirit, it suggests that in the worshipful practice of proclamation and praise the body of believers is infused with and shines forth the light of God's presence.

In his book on discipleship Turner further explores the theme of the church's shining with the beauty of God. There he makes explicit what he implied with the language of the icon—conformity to the Son is a sharing in God. He writes, "Being led by the Spirit means being open to a special relationship with God, a relationship that God initiates. Through this relationship, God nurtures us, guides us, forms us into the image of Christ, making us partakers of the divine nature"—ending with an explicit reference to 2 Peter 1:4.[23] In another passage, Turner weaves together the themes exhibited in the service of worship and in his sermon:

> There is a beauty that God has ordained to be manifested in the covenant community as a holy nation. It is the beauty of the devoted and consecrated life. It is nothing short of beautiful to see how God takes us with all our differences, all of our shortcomings,

22. Turner, "Conformed," 118.
23. Tuner, *Discipleship*, 11.

and fashions a people for divine praise. This is the beauty of those who love and care for one another, and it is the beauty of those who care for the world.[24]

Turner takes the connection between beauty and holiness from Psalm 96:9, which urges the congregation to "worship the LORD in the beauty of holiness." Turner makes a point similar to that of Wesley: our being filled with God's life is nothing other than our material sanctification, which itself is nothing other than our being formed in the image of Christ. By referring to Psalm 96, Turner makes explicit the relationship between participation as beauty, or holiness, and the worship of the community:

> Worshipping in the beauty of holiness entails offering one's self to God for beautification. We bring ourselves into the divine presence so the holiness of God can permeate our beings and beauty be reflected in us. This beautification removes the ugliness of sin and rebellion.[25]

But for Turner, this worship as beautification extends to the practices of the whole church, so that,

> [i]n a profound sense, all we do as God's people is to be done with an attitude of worship. Discipline and doctrine are to be dispensed with an attitude of worship. The order of worship may change, but Bible study, choir rehearsal, even committee meetings and conferences should be done in an atmosphere of worship, for we are not dealing with formal principles and agenda items but with how our personal lives and our common life are to reflect and radiate the beauty of the Lord our God.[26]

Finally, for Turner, the beauty with which the community shines, the glory of God, radiates in the community's bodily practices—this is the very glory God intends for the rest of creation. As he writes, "No glory can be compared with the glory of those who have been redeemed, brought out of darkness into the marvelous light. For this is the glory to which God is bringing all of creation."[27]

24. Ibid., 7.
25. Ibid., 49.
26. Ibid., 51.
27. Ibid., 127.

When these themes are pulled together—themes emerging from the account of worship at Mt. Level and from William Turner's theological narration of the church's life—a particular vision of the church begins to emerge. The church, in all its practices of worship and especially in its practices of praise and preaching, is infused with the life of God so that the body of the church itself glows with the Spirit's radiance, as it is permeated with the beauty of God's holiness. This is no static radiance, for the holiness of the people, which is the holiness of God shining through the people, is displayed in the consecrated life of worship, obedience, and sacrifice, a life that has the particular shape and beauty of Jesus, in whose image the church is being formed through the Spirit. The world sees this radiant beauty and in it sees its own calling and destiny, to share, like this community, in the glory of God.

Like the early Methodist Societies, the life of Mt. Level and its self-understanding as narrated by its pastor raise important questions that give this book its bearings: What is the best way to characterize the kind of participation in God exhibited in the life of this community's worship, preaching, and sacrifice—in its practices? And how is that participation a *bodily* participation? How through the corporate practices of such a community does participation in God become visible? Finally, how can the participation of a community like this in the life of God be extended to the rest of creation?

I begin this book with these accounts of real communities and their self-understanding because nothing is to be avoided more than an account of the church's participation in the life of God abstracted from the real, embodied practices of lived communities. That these communities worship, sing, serve, preach, and practice in various ways their common life, and that they do so with the self-understanding that such living and practicing is the image of God being formed in their lives together—their partaking of God's own life—is the lived reality from which the argument of this book unfolds.

PLAN OF THE BOOK

Let me be more specific about the three important questions raised by my description of early Methodist practice and the worship life of Mt. Level Missionary Baptist Church. These are the questions that guide the argument of this book:

- *First, how should the relationship between the embodied, human practices of these ecclesial communities and the activity of God be understood?* That in these various practices Christ is being formed and God is making his habitation suggests a very close, if not identical, relationship between the divine and human activities involved. Being able to articulate the nature of this relationship is foundational for a theology of church practices.

- *Second, how can these practices and their participation in God be articulated in a way that takes with utter seriousness the clearly embodied nature of these practices, that through "our frame, in our bodies, his beauty shines"?* Through a theological account of church practices, this book seeks to display the material conditions of the church's participation in the life of God. As our look at the Wesleys showed, participation in God—our being conformed to the image of the Son—is not disembodied, but it is the embodied sanctification of a church as God makes it holy.

- *Third, how do these communities relate the rest of creation to God's life as well?* In other words, if these practices are somehow God's taking the church into God's own life, then what do the practices of these communities suggest about their relationship to the world and the world's *telos* in God? I raise this question throughout the book and gesture toward an answer, but a complete discussion of this question presses beyond the scope of this book.

In the end I will argue that these questions are best answered by an account of the church that says the church's participation in God is Christ's practicing himself as the embodied practices of the church, in the Spirit, for the world. Moreover, this practicing, this participation, has a peculiar visibility because it is the Jesus of the Gospels who practices himself in the church; this visibility of the form of Jesus in the church shows the world the shape of its own *telos* in God.

The argument of this book is divided into three parts. Part One, chapters 1 and 2, accomplishes two things. In the first chapter I use the work of James Gustafson and Nicholas Healy to help me display the problem this book addresses, articulated in the questions above, namely, how to offer a theology of church practices in which the concrete materiality of the church's social embodiment is not one side of a problematic dualism (human/divine) while at the same time accounting for how the church is fully constituted by both divine and human activity (the first two questions above); and, how the church community, participating in the life and activity of God in its concrete humanity, relates to the way God's activity establishes and upholds the being of the rest of creation and other social bodies (the third question above). In the second chapter I turn to a discussion of the concept of practices in the work of Alasdair MacIntyre and how that concept has been appropriated by Christian thinkers to understand the nature of the church's social embodiment. My theology of church practices will build upon and critique the important work done by the Christian thinkers I discuss in chapter 2.

After displaying the problem and laying the foundation for my use of the language of practices in Part One, I turn in Part Two, chapters 3 and 4, to the heart of the book—a theological narration of two church-constitutive practices: preaching and Eucharist. As I have already said, a theology of church practices should begin with an exploration of the theology of particular core practices, in this case the liturgically central practices of preaching and Eucharist. In chapter 3 I use Dietrich Bonhoeffer to help me articulate an account of preaching as an embodied church practice of participation in God's life in a way that avoids the problems with the dualistic ecclesiologies characteristic of modernity as described in chapter 1. Similarly, in chapter 4 I use the Dominican theologian Herbert McCabe and his account of the Eucharist as language to show how the practice of Eucharist is an embodied church practice of participation in God's life. When McCabe's account of the Eucharist as language is connected to Bonhoeffer's christological account of preaching, I can begin to show how, because these practices are Christ's own practicing himself, participation in God has a particular shape and visibility.

Having argued that a corrective to modern, dualistic ecclesiologies lies in a christological account of church practices as embodied participation in God, I turn in Part Three, chapters 5 and 6, to take up more fully the question of participation so much discussed in contemporary theology, largely due to the work of John Milbank and the Radical Orthodoxy movement. In chapter 5 I argue that the church's participation in God is misconstrued if it is conceived as an exemplification or intensification of creation *qua* creation's participation in God. The church's participation in God, as an embodied, visible participation, is better understood as the *telos* of creation's participation. How the rest of creation and other social bodies participate in God is given meaning and direction by the church's active, embodied, *practiced* sharing in God's life. Then I turn in chapter 6 to Maximus the Confessor's cosmic Christology in which his accounts of deification as an activity, the simultaneous divine and human constitution of that activity, and the church as the locus and *telos* of that activity give theological density and greater specificity to the language of participation I have used throughout the book and in terms of which I understand church practices. Then the full implications of my argument—that the Church is Christ practicing himself in the Spirit for the world—can be spelled out.

I hope that the argument of this book does justice to the real communities engaged in the practices I am trying to make more intelligible. I also hope that it helps those communities, communities like Duke Memorial United Methodist Church, which my wife and I pastor together, better understand who they are and who their God is and how their life together is life in that God, because participation in God is certainly what John and Charles Wesley thought was going on in the practices of the early Methodists. It is also what William Turner and the people of Mt. Level Missionary Baptist Church think is going on in their worship and preaching. It is what I argue is going on in the church's embodied practices. How this is so, how these church practices are indeed Christ's own practicing himself in the Spirit for the world, and why it matters is what I aim to show in the following pages.

Part One

1

Rediscovering the Embodied Church

THIS BOOK IS ABOUT how church practices are the church's embodied participation in the life of God through the union of our bodies with God's. As I showed in the Introduction, for the Wesleys and the early Methodists we are joined "body, soul, and spirit" with God through the practices of the church, especially the Lord's Supper. Growth in this union occurs through the sociality of the church. For the people of Mt. Level, God inhabits the church's praise and corporate proclamation of the gospel. The Holy Spirit irradiates their common life so that they shine with God's glory like an icon of Christ. These communities press us to begin to think about participation in terms of the peculiar visibility of the church, whether conceived in terms of Wesleyan holiness or in terms of the community as icon.

My description of these two communities raised three important questions: First, how should we understand the relationship between the human activity and the divine activity as these two activities are mutually constitutive of church practices? Second, how can a theology of church practices display the material conditions of the church's participation in God by taking with utmost seriousness the embodied nature of these church practices? Finally, how do church practices, fully embodied and constituted by both human and divine activity, point the rest of creation to participation in God's life?

The fundamental issues these questions address are not new. Part of what I am doing in this book is bringing an ancient way of talking about the church—as participating in God—into conversation with those recent approaches to ecclesiology that talk about the church in terms of corporate practices. Therefore, I begin my approach to the question of the church's participation in God by closely considering Cyril of Alexandria's account of the church in his commentary on the Gospel of John, for Cyril represents just one of those ancient ways of talking about the church's participation in God. The discussion of Cyril serves two purposes. First, Cyril offers a tantalizingly beautiful picture of the church, which shows how an account of the church's participation in God must be thoroughly christological. My hope is that these few pages on Cyril whet the reader's appetite for a deeply christological account of the church's embodied practices that the rest of the book intends to offer. Second, however, Cyril serves as an example of how accounts of the church that are theologically rich and centered on the church's participation in God often do not have the resources to describe the embodied, visible sociality that is the church's life. Thus, the discussion of Cyril opens the door for an engagement with those thinkers who have tried to recover for ecclesiology the church as embodied in its social processes and practices.

CYRIL OF ALEXANDRIA AND THE CHURCH OF THE TRIUNE GOD

The few pages in Cyril of Alexandria's *Commentary on John* that remark upon John 17:20–21 are useful because they clearly and succinctly show the heart of reflection on participation and the church in the patristic era. More importantly, they show how Cyril's reflections on the church are directly related to his theology of the unity of Christ. Since throughout this book it will become increasingly clear that Chalcedonian orthodoxy is crucial for overcoming inappropriate dualisms and for understanding divine and human activity in the practices of the church, I begin with Cyril of Alexandria to give us our first glimpse of a theological account of how the church, through the Father's gift of the Son and the Spirit, participates in the very life shared by these three.

Cyril begins his commentary on these verses by emphasizing the strength of the unity, which Christ expects among those who make up the church, a unity that Christ himself made possible, by comparing the unity of the church to Christ's own unity with the Father. Cyril writes, "He thus expresses his will that in the strength of the holy and consubstantial Trinity, we too should be as it were commingled with one another."[1] Citing Ephesians 2:14–16 in which Paul pronounces the unity of the church as the breaking down of the dividing wall between Jews and Gentiles in the body of Jesus, Cyril remarks that the church is like the union of two people

1. Cyril of Alexandria, *Commentary*, 168.

"moving in Christ" towards the "constitution of a perfect single whole."[2] Cyril is clear, however, that this unity is not a hidden unity, but a concrete unity, lived by the church in its obedient pursuit of the good:

> And this purpose is actually accomplished when those who put their trust in Christ are of one soul with one another and receive as it were a single heart; and that comes from the total affinity which true religion gives, from the obedience which is implicit in faith and from the mind that is set on the good life.[3]

The unity of the church in Christ is, for Cyril, the church's practicing true religion, the concrete obedience of faith and the common pursuit of the good life.

When Jesus says that as "you, Father, are in me and I am in you, may they also be in us" (John 17:21b), Cyril believes that Jesus is moving to a deeper, more profound expression of the church's unity, which is more but not other than the church's obediently practicing a common life of faith. The unity of the church is a unity in the triune God. Cyril explores how this deeper unity, "which does not exclude unity even at the bodily level,"[4] is made possible by the gift of Christ and the Spirit in the church's eucharistic celebration first by reiterating the Christology that has come to be recognized as distinctly his own:

> The Only-begotten has shined on us from the very substance of God the Father; having his own nature and fullness of the one who begat him, he became flesh . . . and mixed himself as it were with our nature by virtue of an inexpressible conjunction and union with this earthly body. So he who is God by nature was called—indeed actually became—a heavenly man. . . . So he was God and man in one. He made a sort of union in himself of two things which are utterly distinct and remote from one another in nature, and thereby made man to share and participate in divine nature.[5]

Several things are worth noting about this passage. As I said in the Introduction, I want to talk about the church as constituted by its practices, and indeed later I will say that the church rightly understood is where Christ practices himself in the Spirit. Here Cyril gives an important safe-

---

2. Ibid., 168–69.
3. Ibid., 169.
4. Ibid.
5. Ibid., 169–70.

guard to any solipsistic understanding of what it might mean for Christ to be practicing himself in the church. The "himself" which is Christ is not a "himself" that is in "himself," but Christ's very self is constituted by his "shining on us from the very substance of God the Father." That is, whatever it means that Jesus performed or practiced his identity as it is recorded in the Gospel narratives or as Christ continues to do in the practices of the church, it cannot be understood in a way that is closed in on itself, precisely because such practicing is the showing forth of a life that comes from another, from the Father. Second, Cyril here expresses succinctly his christological position over-against Nestorius, so much so that Eutychian language, the very thing the Antiochenes feared, creeps into his description when he says that the Son "mixed himself, as it were, with our nature." Nonetheless, Cyril still articulates what is known as Chalcedonian orthodoxy when he writes, "So he was God and man in one. He made a sort of union in himself of two things which are utterly distinct and remote from one another in nature." It is not enough to note that Cyril here reiterates his position on the unity of Christ. What matters is that his notion of participation—how humans have come to share the nature of God—is determined precisely by the hypostatic union. Participation for Cyril is not an abstract, ontological reality, but a soteriological implication of the incarnation in which humans share.

But how do humans share? How is our participation in the divine nature actualized? Cyril's answer to these questions makes one more move that shows how this notion of participation is fully Trinitarian. It is commonplace to say that the church participates in God through the Spirit, and this is usually understood in terms of the distinct *missio* of the Spirit in the church.[6] But Cyril's pneumatological account of our participation does not begin with a discussion of the distinct mission of the Spirit in the church. Instead, he turns to the Spirit's work in the incarnation itself as the only way to make intelligible the Spirit's work in the church. Cyril writes:

6. Reinhard Hütter points out in *Suffering Divine Things* that a lack of a focus on the distinct mission of the Spirit in relationship to the church characterizes the Peterson-Barth correspondence (113). He turns to insights from Eastern Orthodoxy and Luther to offer just such a distinctive mission. In his discussion of Eastern Orthodoxy he notes exactly what we will see here with Cyril: "The specific emphasis on pneumatology in Eastern Orthodox ecclesiology has christological roots. An emphatically pneumatological understanding of Christology avoids the false alternative between a christological and pneumatological grounding of ecclesiology," 118. This will be an important insight in the discussion of Maximus the Confessor in chapter 6 below.

The participation in the Holy Spirit and his abiding presence which began through and in Christ has also been transmitted to us. When he appeared at our level, that is as man, he was the first to be anointed and sanctified, even though in his nature, as he comes from the Father, he is God. With his own Spirit he sanctified his own temple and the whole creation that was brought into being through him, for which the act of sanctification was appropriate. Thus the divine plan was effected in Christ as a beginning of the road whereby we too might receive a share both in the Holy Spirit and in union with God. For we are all sanctified in him in the way that we have just described.[7]

Only after Cyril has said how the Spirit was himself at work in Christ's incarnation, how the Spirit actualized the incarnation, can he begin to say that we ourselves are sanctified by the Spirit just because we participate in that holy flesh of Christ.[8] However one understands the distinct mission of the Spirit in the church, it cannot be viewed as abstracted or separated from how the Spirit worked in Christ's own life. For Cyril, this participation in Christ through the Spirit is constitutive of our own sanctification. We are sanctified as we participate in the sanctified flesh of the man Jesus, whose flesh is nothing other than the body of God. Likewise, that very participation in the flesh of the man Jesus is a sharing in the nature of God, christologically understood.

Finally, Cyril accounts for our sharing in the divine nature in two ways. First, this sharing in the nature of God and the bodily unity of believers occurs through the eucharistic practice of the church in which the church partakes of the very sanctified body of Jesus. "With one body," Cyril writes, "namely his own, he blesses those who believe in him as they partake of the holy mysteries and makes them members of the same body with himself and with one another."[9] We are united bodily, even though we remain distinct, because we share in the one undivided body of Jesus, offered to us in the Eucharist. This eucharistic practice constitutes the church's unity with one another and with Christ through the real par-

---

7. Cyril, *Commentary*, 170.

8. Again, as Hütter says regarding Eastern Orthodoxy, "Actually, then, Christ is conceivable only 'in the Spirit.' This is, the 'being' of Jesus Christ is, in its essence, utterly determined toward the Father. Jesus exists entirely in the communion of the triune God and is completely qualified by this communion; it constitutes his being" (Hütter, *Suffering Divine Things*, 118).

9. Cyril, *Commentary*, 170.

taking of Christ's body; but since this body is also the body of God, any participation in the body of Jesus is at once a participation in the divine nature, for Cyril's own christological formulations will not allow the separation of the divine and human in Christ. If we partake of the body, we partake of God. So, beyond the Trinitarian specificity that Cyril has given to the notion of participation, he here gives it a particular eucharistic determination. He writes, "So if we are all one body with one another in Christ, not simply with one another but clearly also with him who is in us by virtue of his own flesh, then surely we are already both in one another and in Christ. For Christ is the bond of unity, being at once both God and man."[10] In the eucharistic celebration we actually partake of the body hypostatically united to God.

The second way Cyril accounts for our participation in God is through the Spirit's indwelling. "As to our unity in the Spirit, we can follow the same line of reasoning and say that as we all receive one and the same Spirit, namely the Holy Spirit, we are all in a manner conjoined to one another and to God. As individuals we are many but Christ makes the Spirit of his Father, which is his own Spirit, dwell in each of us.... Thus as the power of the holy flesh makes one body of those in whom it is present, in just the same way the 'indwelling' in us all of the one indivisible Spirit makes of us a spiritual unity."[11] He illustrates this unity-by-indwelling in a way that illuminates what he might mean by a "spiritual unity." This unity with the Spirit has a shape, it might be said, which is the practical shape of sanctification; our unity with the Spirit is visible in that in our unity with the Spirit we let the "laws of the Spirit control our lives."[12] The very shape of our lives takes on what Cyril calls the "other-worldly mould of the Spirit."[13] The indwelling of the Spirit, the bond of unity with God and with one another, is visible in the process of sanctification. In this process "we are as it were being changed into another nature, no longer mere men but also sons of God with the title of heavenly men, in that we have been made partakers of the divine nature."[14]

10. Ibid., 171.
11. Ibid.
12. Ibid.
13. Ibid.
14. Ibid.

If there is any fear that this discussion of the Spirit is abstracted from the previous christological discussion, it should be remembered that when we receive the title "heavenly men" we receive the very title that belongs to Christ, "heavenly man," as we saw above. And it was Christ's becoming the heavenly man, in a body sanctified by his own Spirit, that makes possible the Spirit's indwelling in us, making us "partakers of the divine nature."[15] Thus Cyril concludes, "So we are all one in Father, Son and Holy Spirit, one in identity of attitude (to recall what we said at the beginning), one in conformity to the ways of piety, in participation in the holy flesh of Christ and in participation in the one Holy Spirit, as we have said."[16]

Cyril describes the church as participating in the triune God. His account of that participation is controlled by an understanding of the Son's mission to "shine on us" from the very substance of the Father by his union with human nature, a union in which the Spirit plays a constitutive role. For Cyril, our participation in the divine nature, our sharing the life of God, is made possible through the hypostatic union of the divine and human in Christ and the church's partaking of the human, and thus the divine, in the eucharistic celebration. Cyril shows how an appropriate account of participation needs full trinitarian exposition. Furthermore, Cyril shows that our participation is not an ontological abstraction, but is the very activity of partaking of the sanctified body of God. Even in his discussion of the indwelling of the Spirit, Cyril shows that participation is not a static condition but a process of turning toward God and being made a partaker of God's own nature in a way analogous to Christ's own divinity. Cyril does not answer all of the questions that I have raised and will raise as these pages progress—especially since he lacks the resources to talk about the church in its concrete, social embodiment—but he serves as an appropriate entry into the discussion of participation before turning to those who rightly critique the level of abstraction associated with some modern approaches to ecclesiology as these approaches dismiss the concrete human social processes and practices that make the church what it is.

15. For a full discussion of the concept of participation in God in Cyril, see Keating, *Appropriation of Divine Life.*

16. Cyril, *Commentary*, 171.

THE EMBODIED CHURCH AND THE ACTIVITY OF GOD

The peculiar visibility of the church—its very human, embodied sociality—has not always been considered constitutive of the church. James Gustafson argued forcefully in the middle of the last century that ecclesiologies of the modern period characteristically occluded the concrete human dimension of the church, sidelining it, so to speak, by identifying the real essence of the church with a disembodied, hidden relationship with God, thus establishing a problematic dualism. The church is constituted, at least partially, Gustafson argued, by social processes and human interactions, institutional structures and ways of governance that resemble those of other social bodies. Nicholas Healy has more recently reinvigorated this argument, noting that since these "human" aspects of the church are prone to sin, the essentialist and idealistic ecclesiologies of modernity, those depictions of the church that describe the ideal church in theological terms, too easily disregard the very concrete, embodied existence of the church with all its weaknesses and failings.

Here I examine the work of Gustafson and Healy to show why the essentialist ecclesiologies of modernity need to be critiqued in order for me to articulate a theology of church practices grounded in the church's bodily participation in God. Furthermore, looking at their work will help me further refine the three guiding questions of this book: How should the relationship between the divine and human activity in the church be understood? How can an account of the church's participation in God take seriously the church's embodiment? And how do the practices of the church open the rest of creation to the life of God? While in the end I argue that Gustafson and Healy's respective approaches are no more adequate than the so-called "essentialist" accounts they critique, they are nonetheless helpful for putting the embodied social processes and practices that make up the church back on the theological table.

Four questions guide my reading of the work of both Gustafson and Healy:

- How does each one describe the nature of the ecclesiology he is critiquing?

- What alternative ecclesiological proposal does each offer?

- How does each one's account of the church relate to his understanding of the activity of God in the world and the church?

- How does each one understand the church's relationship to other social bodies?

By asking and answering these four questions, I will be able to show why it is important to focus on the material practices that make up the church but also why such a focus, conceived in the way Gustafson and Healy conceive it, is not adequate if the church we are trying to understand and live is the church of the triune God.

James Gustafson's Concrete Church

When James Gustafson wrote *Treasure in Earthen Vessels* in 1961 he was responding to a surge of writings on the church in the previous forty years that would culminate in the reflections on the church of Vatican II. He argued that much of this writing ignored what he calls the human, and thus social, nature of the church. He writes that "the main attention has been given to a doctrinal understanding of the 'essence' of the Church, or to the relation of the Church to the persons of the Trinity."[17] He introduces into discussions of the church what he views as a much-neglected aspect of the church. "Efforts to take the social nature of the Christian community seriously in theological discourse are rare."[18] Thus he focuses on the church "as an historical, human community," employing the insights and tools of social theory to try to understand better how the church "works." Only when this aspect of the church is taken fully into account, he argues, can the theological reductionism of essentialist ecclesiologies be corrected.

The Church as Human Social Processes

How exactly does Gustafson describe the theologically reductive ecclesiologies he is critiquing? In mounting his critique, Gustafson cites a eucharistic account of the church that says that with "the Body of Christ the form of that Body is given and maintained. Church order is the form of the Body. . . . Thus in the Eucharist the Church assumes true form and order in obedience to the Word, but as such that order is not static, but dynamic, not a state but an action."[19] According to Gustafson, the "form"

17. Gustafson, *Treasure in Earthen Vessels*, 1. This looks like a critique of the kind of ecclesiology we have already encountered in Cyril of Alexandria, one given in the theological terms of the Trinity.

18. Ibid.

19. Torrance, *Royal Priesthood*, 72; quoted in Gustafson, *Treasure in Earthen Vessels*, 6.

and "order" of the church should be able to be described sociologically. This eucharistic understanding, he says, ignores a sociological approach to "form" and "order," thus presenting an abstract and ambiguous account of the church, couched in the doctrinal language of theology but ignoring important dimensions of the church (Gustafson would probably make the same critique of Cyril's account above). It is worth quoting Gustafson's critique at length:

> From the point of view of a social analyst a number of questions must be answered before such a statement begins to be meaningful. Is the Body of Christ identical with the historical community of Christians? If it is not identical, precisely what is the relationship? Do the form and order of the body have any reference to historical structures in the life of the Christian community? Or is reference to something more like form or idea in Plato's philosophy? If this is the case how does social order in the Church participate in its "true form" in the Body? From the point of view of a social interpretation the fundamental difficulties of a statement like [the one above] lie in its lack of clarity in the meaning of words and its abstractness. It is removed from what most Christians refer to when they think of the Church, i.e., a body of people, a social movement.[20]

Most fundamentally, Gustafson thinks idealizing ecclesiologies pose a problematic dualism—a bifurcated church—with an essential nature removed from the material, historical, social aspect of the church. "A doctrinal reductionism refuses to take seriously the human elements of the Church's life, or if it acknowledges them it does not explore or explicate them in doctrinal language . . . Many theologians ignore part of their task in ecclesiology, i.e., to make theologically intelligible the human forms and processes that can be understood and interpreted from a social perspective."[21] Gustafson does not deny that theological descriptions of the church are appropriate, but only that those faliling to relate the theological (i.e., ideal) descriptions to the type of descriptions of the church made available through sociological categories cannot do justice to the church's lived, historical existence.

If the theologians fail because they postulate that "a suprahistorical or essential nature of the Church is more real, purer, or of greater value

20. Gustafson, *Treasure in Earthen Vessels*, 7.
21. Ibid., 105.

than its changing social character,"[22] Gustafson points directly to that very social character as that aspect of the church through which God works. For Gustafson, "the Church can be defined as a human community with an historical continuity identifiable by certain beliefs, ways of work, rites loyalties, outlooks, and feelings."[23] As a human community "it is human, and shares many characteristics of other human communities such as nations, trade unions, and professions. As a human community it is subject to various modes of study and interpretation."[24] A little later he defines the church as *"an historically continuous body of persons known as Christians, whose common life is in part institutionalized in churches. The Church is a social entity, with temporal and spatial boundaries."*[25] Gustafson's point is that the church, understood in this way, can be analyzed using the tools and categories of the sociological disciplines used to describe any other human social body.

These remarks indicate how Gustafson thinks the church relates to other social bodies. All human social bodies exist in social processes; in some sense they do the same thing. Rather than focusing on the putative theological uniqueness of the church, Gustafson looks at how the church's social processes are like those of other communities. The church, for instance, "meets some of the same natural needs that life in the family, or the economic order, or educational institution also meets."[26] The church is also an institution and a political community, and thus is ordered by political processes like other communities. As Gustafson says, "[T]he political processes are essentially the same in both the gathering of the men in loyalty to the nation and the gathering of men in loyalty to Jesus Christ."[27] More importantly, the church, like other communities, is "in part designated by the common language" of its members.[28] "Those who know the language belong to the community; those who do not know it are outside. This is as true for the historical Christian community as it is for the German nation, or for the fellowship of physicians."[29] The church

22. Ibid., 110.
23. Ibid., 3.
24. Ibid.
25. Ibid., 6; emphasis in original.
26. Ibid., 8.
27. Ibid., 9.
28. Ibid.
29. Ibid.

is a community of memory and understanding, of interpretation, and of belief and action. In all of these ways, the church is constituted by social processes like other communities.

Gustafson's attempt to recover the humanity of the church, its existence in its concrete social process, involves critiquing modern ecclesiologies for locating the essence of the church in its theological ideality (an answer to the first guiding question). Constructively, Gustafson argues that the church is made up of social and political processes (an answer to the second guiding question). As my very brief description of his approach makes clear, his looking at the church as a human institution constituted by social processes entails an answer to the question of the relationship of the church to other social bodies; it is a relationship of *similarity* (an answer to the fourth guiding question).

The Human Church and the Activity of God

But how does he answer the third question—the most important for an account of the church's participation in God—about the relationship between God's own activity and the social processes that constitute the church, if, as Gustafson maintains, he does not want to abandon theological interpretation in favor of sociological interpretation? Admitting that his own approach can tend toward a sociological reductionism, Gustafson tries to show how the sociological and the theological relate.

Gustafson asks, "[H]ow can the significance of the social processes and elements be theologically understood?"[30] Gustafson's account has argued that the church can be understood as both an institution and fellowship, the objective, institutional structures being necessary to sustain the fellowship, because the "identity of the inner life as Christian depends upon the proper functioning of institutional forms."[31] On the other hand, he writes, "The Church exists only where the meanings objectively carried by the forms are subjectively appropriated and believed by persons. The inner community has a quality of common spirit as these forms provide the center of meaning and faith for personal life and for the common life of Christians."[32] Fellowship refers to this inner life of the community; it refers "to a special aspect of community, namely, the interpersonal, sub-

30. Ibid., 100.
31. Ibid., 102.
32. Ibid., 103.

jective sense of oneness that exists among Christians."[33] The church as institution and fellowship comprise the church's sociological nature.

How the church relates to God's activity is dependent upon this two-sided sociological structure. More specifically,

> The common inner life of the Church is not only the effect of processes of internalization of objectified meaning. It is not only the subjective counterpart to the objective signs and marks of life given in institutional forms. It is *koinonia*, a fellowship given by Jesus Christ and sustained by the activity of the Holy Spirit of God. It is a gift, and not just a natural process. God himself is present among men, and makes himself and his actions known in the common life of the Church. The unity and power of the Church are gifts of God's love and marks of his living presence in the Church.[34]

God makes himself known in this inner, common life of the community, the very common life that constitutes the community's historical continuity. By asserting that "God acts in history,"[35] Gustafson can relate God's activity to the very institutional processes that maintain the fellowship, the common inner life of the church, and thus make God present to humanity. "Christians assert in faith," he writes, "that God has made known his capacity to perform his mighty and his commonplace deeds in the realm of the contingent, and the transitory."[36] For Gustafson, a focus on the human aspect of the church, its objective structures and processes, does not negate the ideal, theological nature of the church. They are not in opposition. He writes that "Christians can affirm the historical community and participate in it in a clear and certain knowledge that its humanness is in the power of God. Precisely the natural community, the political community, the community of language, interpretation, and understanding, the community of belief and action, is the Church, God's people. The human processes of its common life are means of God's ordering, sustaining, and redeeming his people."[37] The social processes that the church shares with other social bodies are the way God works in human lives.

These theological claims are surely right but also seriously inadequate. His earlier critique of essentialist ecclesiologies complained that

33. Ibid., 101 n. 1
34. Ibid., 104.
35. Ibid., 108.
36. Ibid., 109.
37. Ibid., 110.

they cannot relate the language of the "Body of Christ" to the very historical body that is the church. But Gustafson does not try to answer this question, asserting instead, without theological elucidation, that God acts through the processes of the church. This is true, but it is as empty as it is true, unless such action can be described in terms of the action of the particular God whom Christians worship as Father, Son, and Holy Spirit.

Interiority and the Church's Continuity across Time

I leave these theological questions to one side (they will surface again later) and examine more critically what Gustafson means by *human* community. For all his emphasis on concrete human processes, Gustafson's privileging of the interiority of the fellowship as the basis for the church's continuity shows a disregard for the very material processes that he champions. Furthermore, I argue that Gustafson's account of this process of interiorizing common meaning is based on a false account of meaning, and thus on an inadequately human anthropology, one that prioritizes interiority over the material constitution of human life. With this I will argue that Gustafson's own account of historicity becomes as *a*historial as the ideal approaches to ecclesiology he critiques.

While the church is similar to other social bodies in that it exists in universal social processes, its particularity is given in the language embodied in these social processes and internalized by the members of the community, according to Gustafson. This question of particularity is related to the question of historical continuity. What, Gustafson asks, constitutes the "'inner unity' and 'inner continuity' through time" of the church community?[38] The answers to the questions of particularity and historical continuity are the same: "The community of Christians maintains its social identity and inner unity through the internalization of meanings represented objectively in certain documents, symbols, and rites."[39] Of course these rites, symbols, and documents, like the liturgy and the Bible, exist independently of the inner subjectivity of the community's members, but their very independence makes possible "the identifiable community of 'subjects' who make up the Church."[40] And since these subjects are the humans who make up the human community of

38. Ibid., 42.
39. Ibid., 43.
40. Ibid.

the church, Gustafson pays this process of internalization a great deal of attention. While Gustafson asserts the independence and objectivity of the institutional structures of the church (rites, symbols, documents), he clearly prioritizes the inner subjectivity of the community when it comes to historical continuity: "Identity in history and across cultures depends upon internalization of meanings carried *potentially* in these objects. The objects do not constitute the Church unless they inform the purposes of individuals and the ethos of a group. It is the internalization of the particular meanings carried by these objects that distinguishes the life of the Church from that of other communities."[41] Historical continuity and particularity exist in the church's internalization of objective meanings carried in the symbols, rituals, and documents of the church.

Unfortunately, this inner/outer dichotomy is as deleterious to an understanding of the church as an ideal theological account that ignores the human aspect. By focusing on interiority as the center of particularity and continuity, Gustafson unwittingly leaves behind the very concrete, materiality of the human processes to which he claims to draw attention. The institutional aspect (exterior, objective) becomes the vehicle for creating true fellowship, the sharing of a common subjectivity and inner continuity over time, the internalization of meaning made available in the objective symbolism of the church. This is problematic for two reasons. First, it suggests a dualistic anthropology, which has in the last century been seriously challenged, an anthropology stemming at least from Descartes, who in his famous *cogito ergo sum* grounded the surety of individual existence in a putative interiority. It underwent a thoroughgoing critique by Ludwig Wittgenstein in terms of its account of meaning.[42] Gustafson's

41. Ibid., 44; emphasis added.

42. Rowan Williams gives a very brief account of this critique: "Common to a good deal of contemporary philosophical reflection on human identity is the conviction that we are systematically misled, even corrupted, by a picture of the human agent as divided into an outside and an inside—a 'true self', hidden, buried, to be excavated by one or another kind of therapy, ranging from intellectual therapy of the post-Cartesian tradition (the modern 'philosophy of mind', the epistemological struggle) to the psychological therapy of another 'analytic' tradition. . . . Modern ethics and theology alike have been haunted by a presence usually called the *authentic* self: an agent whose motivation is transparent, devoid of self-deception and of socially conditioned role playing. As a therapeutic fiction, this is a construct of great power and usefulness. I suspect, though, that it is also a fiction that is intellectually shaky and morally problematic" (R. Williams, *On Christian Theology*, 239). This critique was inaugurated especially by Ludwig Wittgenstein's *Philosophical Investigations*, especially in his discussion of the impossibility of "private language." It

human community is not human enough precisely because, his claims to the contrary not withstanding, the material processes that make up the church become, in the end, incidental to the shared inner subjectivity that comprises the church's true particularity and historical continuity.

Second, in that this interiority cannot itself be described in material terms, nor can its exact relationship to the objective processes of the church be determined, Gustafson's move to interiority is essentially the positing of a new transcendental ideality, an untouchable area *within* the human, conditioned perhaps by the objective processes of the church, but in the end more determinative of the church's nature than those processes themselves. Gustafson is in danger of substituting the essentialism of the theological approaches he critiques with his own anthropological essentialism, the essence of the church for him being that historically continuous inner fellowship, the very fellowship that distinguishes the church from other bodies. Trade unions, nations, and churches all share similar social processes; what distinguishes them are the particular interiorities of each community in the same way that what distinguishes one Cartesian human from another is that my "I" is not your "I." Gustafson writes,

> The unity of a community at any given time through history is at least bi-polar. On the one hand, it centers in persons who share common meanings and interpretations of experience that come out of the past. On the other hand, it centers in the objective external expressions of these meanings from the past given in art, document, and other signs and expressions of lived experience. These objectifications are not entirely dependent for their existence upon the existence of particular persons in a community. *However, they would have no meaning and significance apart from the internalization of their meaning in persons who make up the community.* The internalization processes are the processes of interaction and mental activity we have interpreted under communication, interpretation, understanding commitment, and action. These objectifications carry the past into the present, and carry the unity of the community through time.[43]

---

will receive much further attention in chapter 4 below. For a very helpful analysis of Wittgenstein's critique of what James C. Edwards calls "Descartes' second major bequest to the philosophical tradition: the identification of the self with a mental substance only contingently embodied in a physical organism," see his *Ethics Without Philosophy*, 185ff.

43. Gustafson, *Treasure in Earthen Vessels*, 136–37; emphasis added. The difference between inner and outer history is a critical aspect of Niebuhr's *Meaning of Revelation*, a work doubtlessly important to Gustafson's own account here.

The unity of the community and its historical continuity depend, for Gustafson, on the internalization of meaning potentially available in objectifications of the past. These objectifications "carry" the past and the community's unity, like a cup carries water, waiting to be internalized, or as, on some theories of language, a word "carries" a meaning.[44]

Gustafson has pointed to the human, historical aspect of church ignored by the theologians who offer us essentialist, ahistorical understandings of the nature of the church. Gustafson's own dependence on what he calls a "bi-polar" account of historical continuity, however, with its prioritization of the inner "I" of the community over the objectifications, those carriers of meaning to be internalized by the "I," issues in a kind of reverse essentialism that cannot account for the formation of real, material bodies by the very social processes he outlines. Are language, communication, and interpretation processes by which objective rites, rituals, and documents, transmit "meaning" through internalization into the inner, shared subjectivity of the members of a community (and what makes this subjectivity shared)? Or are language, communication, and interpretation the very material processes themselves, the bodily interaction of members of the community in a particular way? Gustafson's return to the human and the historical in ecclesiology tends toward the *a*historical prioritization of interiority. It is not human enough in that the inner subjectivity is prioritized at the expense of our bodily participation in the very practices that constitute the community, practices that do not *transmit* meaning, but *are* their own meaning.

Nicholas M. Healy's Divine and Human Church

In my discussion of Gustafson I said that I would leave to one side the theological question about how to understand God's working through the human social processes, partly because I think Gustafson's discussion of this is largely unimportant to the purpose of his account and partly because in his discussion he uses the theologically imprecise language (which he acknowledges) of a "God who acts in history," which, as I suggested, is surely true as far as it goes. I also wanted to leave that discussion until I turned to Nicholas Healy's *Church, World and the Christian*

44. Wittgenstein's *Philosophical Investigations* is a lengthy critique of this account of meaning and its attendant anthropology. Nicholas Lash has shown how this account of language and meaning has unfortunate implications for theology. See his *Theology on the Way to Emmaus*, 95–166.

Life: Practical-Prophetic Ecclesiology, for he offers a more theologically sophisticated account of God's activity in relationship to the church and other social bodies, one more helpful than Gustafson's for clarifying the theological issues at stake. Healy's critique is quite similar to Gustafson's, but his theological proposals deserve special attention.

The Invisible Church of Modernity

Like Gustafson, Healy thinks that ecclesiology in modernity has ignored what he calls the "concrete" church, in favor of reflection on the church's ideal nature, its essence.[45] Modern ecclesiology often posits a bipartite structure to the church. One is the true nature of the church which manifests itself in the other, the everyday visible church. "One of its aspects, the primary one, is spiritual and invisible, often described as the church's 'true nature' or its 'essence.' The other aspect is the everyday, empirical reality of the church, its institutions and its activities. The relation between the two aspects is often described by saying that the primary one 'realizes' or 'manifests' itself in the subsequent one, or that the visible church is the 'expression' of its invisible aspect. Thus a genuine understanding of the expression is contingent upon the grasp of the basic, primary core."[46] The everyday, empirical activities of the church do not constitute the church as church except insofar as they manifest the true, hidden nature of the church. According to Healy, if this dualistic ecclesiology is correct, then theological reflection on the nature of the church can ignore the church's mundane existence.

One of the ways modern ecclesiologies tend to downplay the concrete, empirical activities of the church is by focusing almost exclusively on the eschatological church as the bearer of the church's true nature. He writes, "The characteristics of the heavenly church are described as so thoroughly present within the earthly church that there is little that needs to be said about the latter except to describe how those characteristics are realized."[47] This insufficient distinction, according to Healy, between the "church militant and the church triumphant"[48] leads to an underappreciation of the way the "pilgrim church is concrete in quite a different

45. Most modern theologians fall for Healy in this category. He points to Barth, Rahner, and Tillard. See Healy, *Church, World, and the Christian Life*, 28ff.

46. Ibid., 28.

47. Ibid., 37.

48. Ibid.

way from the heavenly church. It exists in a particular time and place, and is prone to error and sin as it struggles, often confusedly, on its way."[49] Thus, Healy argues, "To the extent that modern ecclesiology is governed by an abstract, rationalistic and overly theoretical approach, it makes it difficult for theologians to acknowledge the realities of the church's concrete identity. . . . Ecclesiology is not a doctrinal theory that can be worked out without close attention to the concrete life of the church."[50]

The Church and the Activity of God

If modern ecclesiology elides the church *in via* with the eschatological church, and thus offers an idealized account of the church to the detriment of an understanding of the church's concrete empirical nature, what does Healy propose instead? Unlike Gustafson, who offers a sociological account of the church before returning to a theological discussion, Healy theologically grounds his account of the human, concrete church. He has a particular, theological reason that justifies, even compels, his turning to the church *in via*.

The first move of his theological argument is to suggest that the church is better understood in terms of *activity* than of *being*. Rather than theoretically beginning with an essentialist account of what the church *is*, Healy wants to point to the activity that constitutes the church. But that raises the question, Who's activity? Against what Healy takes to be Barth's claim that God's activity alone creates the church, he writes:

> [The Church's] identity is constituted by action. That identity is thoroughly theological, for it is constituted by the activity of the Holy Spirit, without which it cannot exist. But it is also constituted by the activity of its members as they live out their lives of discipleship. It is therefore not enough to discuss our ecclesial activity solely in terms of its dependent relations upon the work of the Holy Spirit. The identity of the concrete church is not simply given; it is constructed and ever reconstructed by the grace-enabled activities of its members as they embody the church's practices, beliefs and valuations.[51]

For Healy, the church has a dual constitution; it is constituted by the activity of God but also by the very activity of humans embodying particu-

49. Ibid.
50. Ibid., 50.
51. Ibid., 5.

lar practices that make up the church's concrete visibility. Because it is neither divine activity alone nor human activity alone, but the *concursus* of the divine with the human that makes up the church's activity, ecclesiology "must examine our human activity as it concretely is: thoroughly human."[52] This work will involve the use of the tools of any discipline— sociology, anthropology, history—which the theologian finds helpful in describing the very human concreteness of the church. By understanding the human activity of the church this way in relationship to God's activity, Healy opens the way to both theological and sociological descriptions of the church without fearing what Gustafson feared—theological and sociological reductionism.[53] He writes, "Thus any attempt to reflect upon the concrete church requires much more than, say, a sociological analysis of its empirical identity, although such an analysis may well be useful on occasion, provided that it is properly subsumed within theological discourse."[54] He looks at the embodied, human, social practices that make up the church because there is a distinctive theological reason to do so.

Because of this theological grounding for his looking at the "grace-enabled activity of [the church's] members as they embody the church's practices, beliefs and valuation," the answers to our four guiding questions are intimately related. To the first question, Healy, like Gustafson, critiques idealistic ecclesiologies that fail to take seriously the present, concrete reality of the church's life. Healy's proposal, unlike Gustafson's, already entails an understanding of the relationship between God's activity and human activity in the concrete practices of the church. The *concursus* of the divine and human activity in the socially embodied practices of the church marks for Healy the church's uniqueness in a way that Gustafson's account does not. Of course, like Gustafson, Healy recognizes that the church is unique because its members have unique beliefs and loyalties even though the church shares with other social bodies what Gustafson calls "universal social processes." On the other hand, Healy writes that,

> the church claims, in addition, that it is unique in a theological way. As the Creed implies, the church's activity and being are dependent in some fundamental and special way upon the activity of the Spirit of Christ in its midst. It is the Spirit who makes the

52. Ibid.
53. Ibid.
54. Ibid., 4.

church's witness true and effective, and who upbuilds the church in a way that moves beyond the possibility of human activity. It is this theological uniqueness that is implied in describing the church by means of such phrases as the Body of Christ, *Creatura Verbi*, Temple of the Spirit, and the like.[55]

The church's uniqueness resides both in the unique beliefs and loyalties that distinguish it from otherwise similar social bodies, but also in the "special way the activity of the Spirit of Christ" works in its midst.

Other Social Bodies and the Activity of God

If the church has this uniqueness, how does Healy understand the relationship between the church and other social/religious bodies? Here Healy, in a way, takes back his claim to the uniqueness of the church in that he does not spell out the "special way" in which the Spirit works in the church. In order to understand the church's place in the world, Healy turns to Hans Urs von Balthasar's theodramatics. Healy, via Balthasar, argues for a theodramatic horizon, in which "*everything* is located within the sphere of God's creative and redemptive activity. All human activity is dependent upon the prior activity of God, yet because of our location within the theodrama, we are truly free to play our own part in ways that are in some sense really independent of God."[56] The church has a distinctive role to play in this theodrama. But so do other social bodies. The church is not the only character in the play. As Healy writes, "Human agency is *fully* constitutive of *all* human institutions and bodies, including the church. At the same time, divine agency is *fully* constitutive of all bodies, including those that are non-ecclesial and non-religious. There is nowhere where God is not creatively and redemptively present."[57] This theological move is important for a theological denial of a secular realm outside of God's sphere of activity. It is also important for an account of human activity in which humans can be said to be truly free because God is not another actor on the stage, but upholds all the activity of the drama itself. This theological principle of the non-contradictory relationship between divine and human activity, so that human activity fully is constituted both by the divine and human, is very important and we will have reason to

55. Ibid., 9.
56. Ibid., 66.
57. Ibid., 67.

return to it again. What I want to note here is how, because Healy does not give any particular specification to the way God's activity constitutes, along with human activity, the church, the very uniqueness of the church and its relationship to God's activity is drastically relativized. He writes:

> This has a number of implications for ecclesiology. . . . If God is active everywhere, then all human activity bears some relation to God, and to bracket that relation can only be a temporary move. At the same time, this conception of divine-human *concursus* relativizes in at least one significant way the status of the church and its theological discourse as they relate to to other religious and non-religious bodies. It is indeed the case that the church is different from such bodies both in degree and in kind because the Spirit is active within it in a distinctive manner. . . . Yet the theodramatic horizon suggests that we consider *all* religious and non-religious bodies to be constituted concretely by both kinds of agency, divine and human. . . .
>
> [The church's] identity is thus thoroughly dramatic in form, for it is the embodiment of its struggle to follow, reject or ignore the movement of the Spirit in its midst. Something formally similar can be said of other religious and non-religious bodies, too: the Holy Spirit, human actions that display finitude and sin, as well as grace-enabled action in accordance with God's will—these are constitutive of all human institutions and groups, whether they make any attempt to follow God's will or not. It is within and by means of this confused mix that we make our contribution to the theodrama.[58]

Healy does not spell out the "distinctive manner" in which the Spirit is active within the church, and without such a spelling out it is impossible to know how the church's uniqueness as a body, which Healy affirmed above, is given by its relationship to God and its role within God's drama of salvation. Whereas some describe the church in terms of the distinct *missio* of the Spirit, it is clear that for Healy the Spirit's mission is not distinctive in its relationship to the church.

CONCLUSION

Gustfason and Healy's calling for a return to the church's human practices is an important call to anyone like me who attempts to reflect theologically on the church. In many ways Gustfason's pointing to the embodied

58. Ibid., 67–68.

social processes that constitute the church was one of the most crucial developments in ecclesiology in the last century. It is hard to say whether the language of practices, so prominent today, would have been possible without the recovery he initiated, for the language of practices is meant to point precisely to that aspect of the church sidelined in the modern ecclesiolgies both Gustafson and Healy critique.

Furthermore, their work underlines the importance of the guiding questions raised by my description of early Methodist societies and the worshiping practices of Mt. Level Missionary Baptist Church. Central to each of these men's work is the first guiding question: How should the relationship between the embodied, human practices of ecclesial communities and the activity of God be understood? What Gustafson and Healy are deeply concerned about is the inadequacy of modern descriptions of the relationship of the church to the activity of God just insofar as these ecclesiologies deny the church's embodiment as constitutive of its true nature. In their critique they highlight the centrality of this question for a full ecclesiology that takes seriously the church's embodiment. Thus they also point to the importance of the second question: How can a theology of the church's participation in God be articulated in a way that takes with utter seriousness the embodied nature of the church and its practices? Though not so much concerned with questions of participation, they aim at ensuring that no ecclesiology fails to take seriously the human, and thus embodied, nature of the church. Finally, their mutual concern to show how the church is similar and dissimilar to other social bodies points to the third question: How does the embodied church's activity relate God to the rest of creation—including other social bodies? For instance, Healy's adverting to von Balthasar's theodramatic account of the church suggests that the church is one social body constituted by the Spirit, albeit in a unique but unspecified way, on the stage with other divinely constituted social bodies.

Unfortunately, Gustafson and Healy's usefulness in highlighting the crucial importance of these questions for understanding the church is equaled by their failure to answer the questions in a completely satisfactory way. It may be true that Cyril, as a fifth-century theologian, does not have on his radar screen issues of the church's embodied sociality or the language to express it, but Cyril has something these theologians lack (a lack for which they can't blame their historical location): a robust account of how the particular activity of the triune God constitutes the

43

church. Such an account, especially when it includes a commitment to Chalcenonian Christology, might have saved Gustafson from his own problematic dualism—that is, his locating the true being of the church in its putative interiority over time, thus neglecting the very body of the church he sought to recover. Such an account might have given these writers the language to name *how* embodied human activity and divine activity mutually constitute the church and not just *that* this dual constitution is so. Finally, such an account might have given a way to talk about the distinct way in which the activity of God makes the church what it is, so that it is clear how other social bodies, likewise constituted by the activity of God, are not also church.

Here is another way of naming their deficiency: Gustafson and Healy's respective accounts of the church are not adequate to make sense of the rich practices and self-understanding of either early Methodism or Mt. Level Missionary Baptist Church. The hymns of Wesley are thoroughly christological. When the early Methodists met in their class meetings and when they celebrated the Lord's Supper—both embodied, social activities—they thought they were being sanctified, carried deeper into the life of God through Christ. Mt. Level's image of itself as an icon—an embodied participant in God's glory—would be impossible without a two-natures Christology. Neither of these communities believe that they are simply one among many social bodies constituted by the activity of God, but they believe that they embody the life of God in a way that the rest of the world cannot live without. The way these two communities embody their life together and the way they understand their embodied lives demands a richer theological account of what it means to be church in all its humanity, in all its divinity.

2

Theological Uses of MacIntyre's "Practices"

THE HEART OF THE unfolding argument of this book is that the church's embodied practices *are* the church's participation in God's life. The church's participation in God's life is not a mystical essence or invisible interiority—it is not one side of a dualism. It is corporate and visible. What the church as a body does over time is the church's very life in God.

In chapter 1 I made three steps along the path toward showing how this is so. First, I used Cyril to help show that an understanding of the church as a participant in the life of God does indeed involves the church's embodied practices, especially the Eucharist, while at the same time I used Cyril to lay the groundwork for a fully trinitarian exposition of participation. Second, I pointed to Gustafson and Healy's recovery of the notion of the concrete, embodied church for ecclesiology. They argue forcefully that the church is an embodied community that should be described in terms of its corporate activities and practices. Finally, I argued that Gustafson and Healy's failure to answer crucial questions about how God's activity relates to the church's corporate activities and practices highlights what is necessary for a theological articulation of the church's practices as embodied participation in God—an account of the relationship between the divine and human activity in the church's practices, a determined focus on the church as an embodied community (which Gustafson gave with one hand and took away with the other), and an account of how the church, constituted by divine and human activity, relates to the rest of creation, including other social bodies, and relates creation to God.

The next step requires offering some specificity about my use of the language of "practices." As I suggested in the Introduction, the use of this language to describe the Christian life and the life of the church is growing in popularity and importance; it is also growing more diffuse.

Both Gustafson and Healy pointed to a consideration of practices as the church's concrete embodiment. Gustafson spoke of "human social processes" and Healy of "practices, beliefs, and valuations," but neither gave an account of what exactly they meant by these terms. Yet the language is crucial to my argument that the church's performance of itself and its being taken into God's own life takes place in and as the embodied social practices that make the church what it is. In this chapter I make clear what I mean by my use of the language of practices and show how some theologians have appropriated that language to make sense of the church's life as it relates to the life of God.

The philosophical discussion around practices has not been monolithic. The philosophers Pierre Hadot, Michel Foucault, Michel de Certeau, Alasdair MacIntyre, and others have contributed to the conversation about practices as it has been taken up by Christian theologians.[1] My use of the language of practices draws chiefly from MacIntyre. His conception of a corporate practice, articulated as one aspect of his broader argument for the necessity of virtues for a coherent understanding of the moral life and for his broader concept of tradition, is useful for understanding Christian practices and has been influential on those who have sought to articulate how the church itself and Christian life are constituted by embodied, social practices. For these reasons, I consider Alasdair MacIntyre's account of social practices before turning to some Christian thinkers who have made use of it. What follows is not so much a critical engagement with MacIntyre, as an outline of his concept of practice in order to prepare us for a critical engagement with those who have been influenced by him.

ALASDAIR MACINTYRE'S ACCOUNT OF PRACTICES

Alasdair MacIntyre argues that the post-Enlightenment era is one of moral incoherence since there is no longer a coherent tradition of morality in which our moral notions make sense. He attempts to recover a coherent moral tradition by returning to the classical tradition of the virtues, especially as expressed by Aristotle. Recognizing, however, that *prima facie* the tradition itself is not monolithic, but comprises many different conceptions of virtue, he nonetheless argues that there is a way to

---

1. See Bass, *Practicing Congregation*, 68, for a helpful summary of different perspectives on the use of the language of practices by these various philosophers and Christian thinkers.

distinguish the core beliefs about virtue that belong to the tradition from those that do not. He begins by arguing, "One of the features of the concept of virtue which has emerged with some clarity from the argument so far is that it always requires for its application the acceptance for some prior account of certain features of social and moral life in terms of which it can be defined and explained."[2] It is in the process of arguing for a core concept of the virtues that MacIntyre articulates his concept of a social practice in terms of which virtue can be at least partially understood (to fully understand virtue also requires the concepts of narrative and tradition). It is important to remember that MacIntyre's account of social practice is in service of his argument for a core conception of the virtues, for when it becomes appropriated by the Christian thinkers we will discuss below it becomes largely separated from MacIntyre's conception of virtue, partially I think because of the perceived incompatibility of his account of virtue (at least as presented in *After Virtue*) with Christianity.[3]

That very notion of a particular type of practice is perhaps the most quoted of all of MacIntyre's work. It is a complex definition articulated succinctly:

> By a "practice" I am going to mean any coherent and complex form of socially established cooperative human activity through which goods internal to that form of activity are realized in the course of trying to achieve those standards of excellence which are appropriate to, and partially definitive of, that form of activity, with the result that human powers to achieve excellence, and human conceptions of the ends and goods involved, are systematically extended.[4]

There are several aspects of this definition of practice that are worth pointing out.[5]

---

2. MacIntyre, *After Virtue*, 186.

3. For a critical engagement of MacIntyre's account of virtue from a Christian theological perspective, see Hauerwas and Pinches, *Christians Among the Virtues*, 55–69. They write, "We cannot, then, begin with Aristotle's virtues and fill in the gaps with Christianity, nor can we, as Christians, defend virtue first and Christianity later, the strategy we find prevalent in MacIntyre" (68). In this critique they are following John Milbank.

4. MacIntyre, *After Virtue*, 187.

5. Similar accounts of MacIntyre's notion of practice can be found in Ballard, *Understanding MacIntyre*, 11–17, and in Kallenberg "Master Argument of MacIntyre's *After Virtue*," 21–22.

Four Aspects of a Practice

First, a practice is a "socially established cooperative human activity." A practice is something people do together; it cannot be done in isolation from the community of practitioners, even if it can be done alone. That is, painting is a practice—there is a community of painters that extends across time with which a painter is in conversation—even if the painter is actually executing his art alone in his study (this aspect is important for my argument that preaching is a practice, especially since most preaching is usually considered something the preacher does *by him or herself*). If we think back to the "social processes" of Gustafson's account of the church, we see that he sees these processes in terms of their human, social constitution. The political processes and the modes of communication within the church are cooperative human activities. This cooperative human activity is also what Healy has in mind when he talks about the human activity that constitutes the church.

Second, a practice, as a cooperative human activity, has "goods internal to that form of activity." A good internal to a practice (MacIntyre's example is chess)[6] is the performing or participating in the practice itself, so that the practice and all that constitutes it becomes, to some extent, an end in itself. It is done for its own sake. In MacIntyre's example, a child has not yet learned to appreciate the practice of chess if the child is still playing because he has been promised candy. Furthermore, goods internal to a practice are those goods unavailable except through participating in the practice itself. There is another important aspect to the goods internal to a practice. External goods are characteristically the possession of someone—a trophy or prize money, for example. They are "characteristically objects of competition."[7] On the other hand, MacIntyre writes that "[i]nternal goods are indeed the outcome of competition to excel, but it is characteristic of them that their achievement is a good for the whole community who participate in the practice."[8] This aspect again will be important for our discussions of preaching and the Eucharist, because the goods internal to those practices are partially definitive of the practices themselves, and when goods external to those practices begin to predominate the practices themselves have become corrupted. The extent

6. MacIntyre, *After Virtue*, 188.

7. Ibid., 190.

8. Ibid., 190–91.

to which these practices can be understood as participation in the life of God will depend on how the goods internal to the practices can be seen as God's activity of taking the church into God's own life in terms of the particular practices themselves.

Third, a practice has "standards of excellence which are appropriate to, and partially definitive of, that form of activity." The goods internal to a practice are measured by a standard of excellence also partially constitutive of the practice and independent of the subjectivity of participants in the practice. That is, the achievement of goods internal to a practice can, to some extent at least, be objectively measured according to the shared standards of excellence. As MacIntyre writes, "A practice involves standards of excellence and obedience to rules as well as the achievement of goods. To enter into a practice is to accept the authority of those standards and the inadequacy of my own performance as judged by them. It is to subject my own attitudes, choices, preferences and tastes to the standards which currently and partially define the practice."[9]

Finally, the shared standards of excellence along with the "human powers to achieve excellence, and human conceptions of the ends and good involved, are systematically extended" through the history of the practice. Over the history of a practice the community of participants will adjust and advance both the standards of excellence and the goods achieved in response to the ability of the participants to participate better in the practice. As the practice develops, new, unanticipated internal goods might be discovered, while corruptions of the practice will need to be avoided and corrected if the systematic extension of the practice is to continue. MacIntyre notes that "the institutionalization of a practice is both necessary for the survival of a practice but also contributes to the corruption of the practice particularly because institutions are usually concerned with external goods."[10] Both Gustafson and Healy have argued that ideal depictions of the church ignore the institutional structures of the church; but they, with MacIntyre, show that any approach to the church that deals with the church's constitutive web of cooperative

9. Ibid., 190. While Christians strive for excellence in their practice, the internal goods of Christian practices are not "outcomes of competition to excel." For a helpful discussion of appropriate excellence in Christian practice, see Jones and Armstrong, *Resurrecting Excellence.*

10. MacIntyre, *After Virtue,* 194.

human activities cannot ignore the institutional structures of the church.[11] While practices systematically extend themselves, they also must guard against withering from corruption, corruption that usually comes about by an undo focus on external goods.

PRACTICES IN CHRISTIAN THOUGHT

These four aspects of MacIntyre's concept of practice are important for understanding the purposeful, cooperative human activities that constitute societies and social bodies. MacIntyre offers a theoretical account, which many have found congenial for speaking more specifically about those very human activities that constitute the church. When theologians and Christian thinkers have appropriated MacIntyre, certain aspects of his concept get emphasized while certain others are downplayed. Theologians have been uncomfortable with the notion of a practice being so focused on the extension of human excellence, especially since ecclesial practices are not dependent on human excellence alone but on God's gracious self-giving. While MacIntyre has articulated a concept of practice in the course of an argument about the nature of human virtue, his account has been largely appropriated for its usefulness in describing and understanding practices themselves, those social processes and practices that constitute the human activity of the church.

Theological Appropriation I—James Wm. McClendon Jr.

James McClendon, in the middle section of *Ethics*, the first volume of his systematic theology, explicitly appropriates MacIntyre's conception of practice, as outlined above, to make sense of what he calls the second strand of Christian ethics, the social strand, the communal context of Christian ethics. McClendon divides his discussion of ethics into three strands for heuristic purposes, repeatedly warning that the strands are essentially intertwined. The first strand, or the sphere of the organic, discusses ethics in terms of human embodiment and what it means for ethics to be about how embodied humans live. The second strand, or the sphere of the communal, argues that all embodied humans are by nature social beings and thus ethics has a distinctly communal orientation. The

11. As we will see in the next chapter, Bonhoeffer's linking the practice of preaching with ordination is one example of practices being sustained more broadly by institutional structure.

final strand, or the sphere of the anastatic, discusses how the hope of new life in the resurrection transforms both the bodily and the social strands of ethics. No one of the three can be understood apart from the other. MacIntyre's notion of practice plays a determinative role in McClendon's articulation of the second, social strand. Thus, McClendon exemplifies the tendency of Christian appropriations of MacIntyre's notion of practice to use the concept less for understanding the nature of virtue and more for understanding the nature of social life.

This look at McClendon's work examines three points relevant to the present discussion. First, I show the particular way he emphasizes MacIntyre's account of practice and how he connects MacIntyre's account to the theological and biblical account of social life that he wants to give; second, I look at how McClendon's use of the concept of practices helps him account for the social constitution of the church; finally, I show how this concept allows him to give an account of the relationship between the church and the world.

PRACTICES AND THE INTRINSIC SOCIALITY OF HUMAN LIFE

McClendon highlights the notion of goods internal to a practice, that is, the intrinsic value of a practice itself, the need of skills (virtues) to participate in a particular practice, and the necessity of a broader social narrative, which provides the space for the web of practices making up a particular society or social body. First, McClendon's emphasis on the intrinsic good of a practice helps him relate his account of the social strand of ethics to the organic strand and also makes something like practices "natural" to human society. He writes, "Life, we say, is worth living, and part of what we mean is that the struggles entailed by such a world as this are worthwhile independent of the ultimate rest that will come when all is over."[12] For McClendon, the living of life is inescapably related to the participation in practices precisely because humans are embodied creatures, biological members of a species who "grow, mate, reproduce, encounter threats to life and opportunities for delight, enjoying their drives, needs, and capacities in a given environment, and must sooner or later mature, age, and die"—all those things implied by our being embodied humans.[13] Our embodied lives, worth living in themselves, are lived in

12. McClendon, *Ethics*, 168.
13. Ibid.

cultures formed by social practices; thus the inescapability of the social strand. McClendon expands the notion of the internal goods of practices to account for the social constitution of all human life and its own worth. Second, that human life embodied in social practices is worth living implies that this life is worth living well; thus, McClendon turns to a brief discussion of virtues, those "skills for living [that] are embedded in the several stories of which we are a part and so cannot be understood apart from these stories."[14] Virtue receives its fullest discussion in McClendon's account of the bodily strand precisely because virtues are the skills necessary for living the kind of embodied life that we live, a life with needs, desires, and capacities.[15] But a discussion of embodied virtues alone can become abstract because particular virtues "have their home in connection with particular practices whose pursuit evokes exactly those virtues," even though some virtues are evoked in every practice.[16] Thus MacIntyre's notion of practice allows McClendon to account for how embodied virtues are lived and exercised in relationship to particular, concrete social practices and not in the abstract. Finally, McClendon points to the narrative character of society as the necessary condition for the meaningful relationship among different practices. He writes:

> There is no single form of social whole to be designated "society." The wide variety of practices would have made that unlikely, for differing practices will require differing institutions for their embodiment. Nomads will have no architecture; warring clans will lack the sophisticated practices of peace. What *is* indispensable for making any society (or culture or community) *one* society is that it shall have a narrative tradition whose function is to provide a setting for the several practices of that society, a web that unites them in a single meaning.[17]

In these three ways then, McClendon gives particular emphasis to different aspects of MacIntyre's concept of a social practice in order to account for the social constitution of all human life, especially of different societies and communities, as the grounding of his claim that Christian ethics has an indispensable social dimension

14. Ibid., 169.

15. Ibid., 104–9.

16. Ibid., 169–70.

17. Ibid., 172. Note how the appeal to continuity and particularity does not need, as in Gustafson, an account of transcendental interiority.

PRACTICES AND THE SOCIALITY OF THE CHURCH

McClendon has been influenced by the work of Jacques Ellul and John Howard Yoder, and sees with them that the biblical concept of "principalities and powers" is more adequate than narrow notions of original sin and the fall to account for the situation of the world's rebellion against God's lordship. These biblical principalities and powers are God's fallen, rebellious creatures that "may be identical with the empire and its lords"—that is, "they are linked with particular nations, that is to say with *politics* and *society*."[18] These powers are in conflict with the reign of Christ, and yet "wherever Christ's victory is proclaimed, the corrupted reign of the powers is challenged, and yet the powers remain in being."[19] In a significant move McClendon asserts that "*principalities and powers are none other than the social structures we may also identify as (MacIntyrian) practices.*"[20] That is, MacIntyre's concept of a social practice is useful not only for understanding the undeniable social constitution of human life; it is helpful for understanding the Bible's suggestion that the social constitution of human life is corrupted and redeemed, rebellious against God's reign and yet conquered by the victory of Christ. The social constitution of human life, embodied within a web of social practices, finds its place in the theological narrative of God's creating and redeeming the world as those biblical "powers and principalities" with which Christ conflicts and over which he conquers. That conquering means the possibility of human social existence directed toward God's reign, rather than away; the powers and principalities are not all bad, especially when viewed as redeemed. As the Christian confronts the world of powerful practices, the Christian must remember that "in the time between the resurrection and final coming of Christ, [these powers] remain in an ambiguous state, and thus they delimit and define the social morality of Jesus's followers, who will have to encounter in the form of these powers crosses of their own."[21] These "powerful practices," the principalities and powers that constitute human social existence, create the context in which Christians live and witness.[22]

18. Ibid., 174.
19. Ibid., 175.
20. Ibid., 173; emphasis in original.
21. Ibid., 175.
22. Ibid., 173.

But if these practices constitute *all* human social existence, then McClendon must be able to describe the life of the church in terms of these practices, these powers and principalities, as well. He needs to show "how similar structures constitute community for Christians as well."[23] He does this by focusing on the Christian covenant meal, the Lord's Supper, as indicating the powerful practice of community formation. McClendon writes, "At the fundament of missionary, gentile Christianity, there is a rite not magical, not even (in many usual senses of the term) 'sacramental'— but moral and ethical first of all; that is, aimed at shaping the common life of Christian community."[24] His description of the meal as a practice is worth quoting:

> Here we see an exact way in which the "religious" life of Christians is inseparable from their moral formation. It is a way that escapes the sweep of standard modern ethical theory. For it is not that the act of communion in the Lord's supper provides the church with motives for good behavior as emotivists might concede, or that this act changes the balance of utilitarian goods for its communicants. Rather the meal is part and parcel of a *practice* . . . which we might roughly name the practice of *establishing and maintaining Christian community*. The "rules" for the meal are among the constitutive rules for the practice. . . .
>
> What then of the powerful practice of Christian community with its imbedded symbolic elements of baptism and Lord's supper? So far we have seen a practice as a way of giving social shape to Christian life. As a practice, we know it must have its end and its lawlike means, and it must exist only by way of the intentional participation of "the players," its members. Their goal-directed participation will evoke the excellences of the practice itself, and enhance its progress. But in keeping with what has just been said, we must also understand our churchly practice as an existing *power*. . . . To think of the church as a practice reminds us of all the inspiring things the New Testament says about it. . . . Yet to think of it as a power should also remind us of other (inspired, though less inspiring) utterances also in our New Testament: the Church Christ died for is, alas, one he may spew out of his mouth (Rev 3:16). To see the church as a set of *powerful practices* is to turn from dogmatic blindness to the historical realities of the church.[25]

23. Ibid., 211.

24. Ibid., 216.

25. Ibid., 216, 218; emphasis in original.

McClendon ties MacIntyre's concept of a social practice to a theological account of the church as constituted by a web of social practices that are also powers—that have the possibility of corruption and rebellion. McClendon's use of MacIntyre allows him to articulate in a theological way the concern of both Gustafson and Healy—to turn from idealistic depictions of the church, what McClendon has called "dogmatic blindness," and to see the church in its concrete, human dimension, the "historical realities of the church." McClendon has begun to pave the way for a discussion of the church as constituted by a web of practices, one that does not dismiss the embodied, material nature of the church's social practices and one that finds in these very practices the church's practicing its own identity in the world.

PRACTICES AND THE RELATIONSHIP BETWEEN THE CHURCH AND THE WORLD

By employing the concept of practices, McClendon is able to articulate an understanding of the realtionship between the church and the world, for as he says, "the church-world relation is intrinsic to Christian existence."[26] To show this relationship, McClendon returns to the early church from which he drew his understanding of the Lord's Supper. After examining how early Christian practices of witness and evangelism confronted the powerful practices that constituted the empire in which the early church found itself, McClendon concludes that what is required is a "clearer vision of the way the concrete practices [of the church] overflow into engagement with society."[27] The use of the word "overflow" is interesting here. Continuing with the example of community building, he suggests that Christians, having learned the skills of faithful community building in the practices of the church, will be able to use those same skills as they participate in other societies and communities, in their families, schools, local communities, etc. In a way, McClendon is suggesting that Christian practices are portable. As he writes, once again using the word "overflow," "Disciples will share in the common life and practices of the church. They will also share other commonalities with other neighbors, and in those settings Christian ways can overflow into the wider society."[28] For

26. Ibid., 230.
27. Ibid., 234.
28. Ibid., 235.

McClendon, the distinctive Christian social witness, that is, the church's engagement with the world—that society constituted still by rebellious powers—is "conveyed by example more than by precept."[29] The witness of the church's material, constitutive practices can "overflow" into other communities; faithfully lived, these ecclesial practices can have an effect on the practices of other communities. In McClendon's words, they can "overflow into the wider society." The church is no different from other social organizations of human life, according to McClendon, in that it is constituted by a web of social practices. The difference is that the church seeks to live its practices in a way faithful to the Kingdom of God, which is yet to come even while it lives in the midst of conquered though still rebellious practices and powers. The faithful living of Christian practices can witness to the world of the coming reign when all powers will resume their ordered place in God's creation, while at the same time these practices can actually affect those very powers through the "overflow" possibility of Christian witness.

McClendon is addressing the very questions crucial to the argument of this book. An evaluation of McClendon's contribution will wait until I have discussed another Christian appropriation of MacIntyre's work. Suffice it to say that in the above descriptions it is hard to see how or whether God himself is involved in the powerful practices of the Christian community and how that involvement differs from God's involvement in the powerful, rebellious practices of the world, even though McClendon claims that "it is *not* being said that God comes in strand three while strand two is merely human morality. That is not the sense of the strands. God as God is present to us in every strand, every dimension of our existence— as nature's Numen, as society's Web, as the resurrection's adventurous Ground."[30] If the church's practices are the church's participation in the life of God, then there must be some unique way—there must be some uniquely *trinitarian* way—that the church's divine-human constitution, its embodied participation in God, differs from how the rest of creation and creation's rebellious powers relate to God's activity.

29. Ibid., 237.
30. Ibid., 187.

Theological Appropriation II—Craig Dykstra and Dorothy Bass

Craig Dykstra and Dorothy Bass have, in a number of essays and projects, employed Alasdair MacInyre's concept of a social practice to make sense of the Christian life and the activity of the church. Because of their influence, there has been over the last few years a proliferation of books and articles on Christian practices, most of which take their cue from MacIntyre.[31] In an earlier essay by Dykstra[32] and in an essay together,[33] they have led the way in theorizing the theological reception and transformation of MacIntyre's "practice" so that it might be useful for understanding Christian practices in general. They self-consciously move beyond MacIntyre to show how the language of practices can help us understand what it means to live an abundant life in response to God's grace.

In that early essay, Dykstra notes that a notion of practices is indispensable for understanding our own lives in community. "Our identities as persons," he writes, "are constituted by practices and the knowledge and relationships they mediate. Some of these are so central to who we are that we cannot give them up without being transformed. Correlatively, communal life is constituted by practices. Communities do not just engage in practices, in a sense, they *are* practices."[34] Thus Dykstra is making a claim similar to McClendon's, that human communities are constituted as communities precisely by their communal practices. Having recognized with MacIntyre how crucial practices are for making sense of the lives of communities, Dykstra also recognizes that the life of Christian community, because it is "a form of life that claims to bear intimacy with God," cannot be understood merely in terms of MacIntyrean practices insofar as, for MacIntyrean practices, God does not necessarily matter.[35]

So how do Dykstra and Bass reconceive practice? They offer a succinct definition: "By 'Christian practices' we mean *things Christian people do together over time to address fundamental human needs in response to and in light of God's active presence for the life of the world*."[36] There

---

31. The two books most directly related to the practices "movement" in Christian theology, both of which are collections of essays, are Bass, *Practicing Our Faith*, and Volf and Bass, *Practicing Theology*.

32. Dykstra, "Reconceiving Practice," 161–82.

33. Dykstra and Bass, "Theological Understanding," 13–32.

34. Dykstra, "Reconceiving Practice," 174.

35. Ibid., 174.

36. Dykstra and Bass, "Theological Understanding," 18; emphasis in original.

are two aspects to their account that are particularly important. First, Christian practices deal with fundamental human needs. While this is descriptive of Christian practices, it is also a theological norm that goes beyond MacIntyre. Because practices meet fundamental human needs, their "descriptions of Christian practices contain within them normative understandings of what God wills for us and for the whole creation and of what God expects of us in response to God's call to be faithful."[37] Through these practices Christians "cooperate with God" in meeting the full range of challenges of human existence.[38] When Christians honor the body, embrace death well, show hospitality to the stranger, and rest on the sabbath, they are engaged in an *imitatio dei*, an imitation of the God who himself has done all of these things. Thus, they say, whoever has done these things has "in a sense, shared in the practices of God."[39] The sense in which Dykstra and Bass understand those who participate in Christian practices to share in the practices of God is very precise: Christian practices are performed in light of and in response to God's active presence in the world.

Second, Christian practices have an important epistemological dimension. They have to do with how we come to know God and creation. This is a point Dykstra makes clear in the earlier essay, and which he and Bass pick up in their later account. "Christian practices . . . involve a profound awareness, a deep knowing: they are activities imbued with the knowledge of God and creation."[40] By being, as they say, "truly attuned to the active presence of God for the life of the world," Christians come to understand the world better as that which God loves and recreates; moreover, they come to a deeper knowledge of the triune God. For instance, by keeping sabbath and resting, Christians learn in an embodied way that the running of the world is not dependent on their own productivity, but on the faithfulness of a redeeming God. By adding these two dimensions, among others, to the social and historical understanding of practice they have adopted from MacIntyre, Dykstra and Bass argue that Christian practices are a "constituent element in a way of life that becomes incarnate

---

37. Ibid., 22.
38. Ibid.
39. Ibid., 23.
40. Ibid., 24.

when human beings live in the light of and in response to God's gift of life abundant."[41]

If we want to use this conception to talk not only of practices like hospitality and honoring the body, but of worship, proclamation, and the Lord's Supper—core practices that constitute the community called church—is describing these as practices done "in light of and response to" God's presence and activity saying enough? Surely it is right as far as it goes. But does it help us understand *how* the church comes to share the activity of God? Does it suggest in what way we come to *know* the triune God? This way of talking about practices—"in light of and in response to"—suggests that the activity of God for the life of the world is happening somewhere other than in the practices of the church, so that through the church's practices the church must find where God is working, and join with God, cooperating, so to speak, in meeting human needs.[42] This way of thinking about practices is useful but not entirely adequate if one wants to make sense of the real mystery of the church as the body of the Son, vivified by the Spirit, sharing the very life of God in anticipation of its eschatological fulfillment—the mystery named by Cyril of Alexandria and embodied in the life and self-understanding of early Methodist communities and Mt. Level Missionary Baptist Church.

CONCLUSION

Here, then, is my fundamental critique of the way MacIntyre's account of practices has been appropriated by Christian theologians to make sense of the church and the Christian life. Neither Dykstra and Bass's nor

41. Ibid., 21.

42. This understanding of joining God where God is perceived to be working was popular in the literature of evangelism and missions in the second half of the twentieth century and is still current today, though it has been appropriately critiqued. Leslie Newbigin writes, "This necessary emphasis on the fact that the mission is God's and not ours can be misunderstood. The World Missionary Conference at Willingen in 1952 laid great stress upon this. Following that meeting there was much use of the phrase *missio Dei* (God's mission) in the missionary writing—especially of the 1960s. But this phrase was sometimes used in such a way as to marginalize the role of the church. If God is indeed the true missionary, it was said, our business is not to promote the mission of the church, but to get out into the world, find out 'what God is doing in the world,' and join forces with him. And 'what God is doing' was generally thought to be in the secular rather than in the religious sectors of human life" (Newbigin, *Open Secret*, 18). It has also been critiqued by John Howard Yoder. See Yoder, *For the Nations*, 237–45.

McClendon's account of church-constitutive Christian practices shows how in these very practices the activity of God is one with the human practices themselves so that it can be rightly said that these practices, constitutive of the church, are the church's sharing in the life of God, in a way significantly different from the way God's activity upholds all human activity, even that activity outside of the church. Dykstra and Bass come close. They rightly suggest that in these practices we share in the activity of God. But they seem to be saying that the activity of God is meeting human need in general and that is what is being done through these Christian practices, so that Christian practices are the church's cooperation with God in meeting human need. McClendon also says that God is present to every aspect of human existence and experience, which of course implies God's presence to church-constitutive practices. But how this is the case, in terms of the language appropriate for speaking about the activity of the God who is Father, Son, and Holy Spirit, is not exactly clear. If one wants to think about the church in terms of its very concrete, human, material existence, as it is embodied in the practices of the church, as I do, while maintaining the distinctive emphasis of the Christian tradition as exemplified in the work of Cyril of Alexandria—that through these practices God is sharing God's own life with the church—then one must go beyond the very helpful steps that McClendon, Dykstra, and Bass have made in understanding how the material social practices of the church relate to God's activity of being Father, Son, and Holy Spirit.

What I seek is this: a theological account of ecclesial practices appropriate to the claim that in the practices of the church the church is practicing its own identity as that community which God is sanctifying by taking it, through those very practices, into a participation in God's own life as Father, Son, and Holy Spirit. Thus, whatever theological account we give of ecclesial practices will need to be given in terms of the activity of the triune God to redeem the world, and not in the imprecise language of God's generic presence to and activity in the world. Furthermore, how we understand God's working in the practices of the church—how the church is participating in the life of God—is crucial to understanding how the church relates to the world. Each of the authors we have looked at in this chapter proposes a way to understand the relationship between the church and the world. But since they have not adequately articulated how God is working in the very material practices of the church to redeem the church and the world, they have not given convincing accounts of how the church relates to the rest of creation.

In Part Two, chapters 3 and 4, I examine two specific practices that, among other related practices, constitute the church as church. Those are the practices of preaching and Eucharist. By looking at these practices in theological detail, I will begin to make an argument for how in the material practices of the church—the embodied human activities that comprise the activity of the church—the church is participating in God's own life.

PART TWO

3

Preaching as a Practice of Participation

Dietrich Bonhoeffer's Theology of Preaching

IN THIS BOOK I am offering a theological account of ecclesial practices appropriate to the claim that in the practices of the church the church is practicing its own identity as that community which God is sanctifying by taking it, through those very practices, into participation in God's own life as Father, Son, and Holy Spirit. Such an account will require at least three things. First, it will require a way to talk about how the activity of the church is constituted by both divine and human activity in a way that is distinct from God's activity in the rest of creation. Second, it will require attention to the church's embodied corporate practices as the locus of the *concursus* between the divine and human activity. Third, such a theological account of the divine and human activity as mutually constitutive of the church's embodied practices will entail an understanding of how the church relates to the world.

The language of church practices is helpful in talking about the church's social embodiment. I do not intend to enumerate all the practices of the church that could be considered—indeed, the list would be contested. I will look, rather, at the practices of preaching and Eucharist, the two practices that for most churches make up the weekly rhythm of liturgy. How to understand these specific practices theologically as embodied practices of participation in the life of God lays the foundation for a theological narration of other Christian practices.

THE PRACTICE OF PREACHING?

This chapter explores the church's practice of preaching. In most churches preaching happens on a weekly basis. The preacher, having written the sermon in the study, ascends the pulpit on Sunday morning and delivers a message, the sermon, making both oral and aural what has been written. With the Eucharist it is more obvious, but with preaching the question might need to be asked: Why is *this* activity to be considered an ecclesial practice, especially if practices are essentially social, as I argued in the previous chapter?

In his book, *Improvisation: The Drama of Christian Ethics*, Samuel Wells articulates an account of Christian ethics in terms of theatrical improvisation. In this way he takes the concept of an ecclesial practice and infuses it with the necessary adaptability to context and ever new situations. The notion of improvisation allows him to articulate the importance of adhering to the living tradition of the church for theological ethics and Christian life, with the understanding that that tradition must be flexible and light-footed enough to be practiced in unanticipated situations, situations that call for more than recitation and repetition. He expresses his frustration that improvisation is usually only considered in relationship to preaching, noting that,

> [w]hen a constructive interest in improvisation is taken, attention often quickly focuses on preaching. Preaching is a vital aspect of worship, and is an important practice in the shaping of the church. But to focus on the preacher as the one who improvises on the scriptural text is to miss two significant dimensions that this study seeks to highlight. One is that improvisation is not primarily about words: the first two practices I note, forming habits and assessing status, are not primarily cerebral or verbal practices. The second is that improvisation is a corporate activity: preaching always presupposes a period of corporate discernment and embodiment, which in most services lasts little longer than the time it takes for the preacher to return to the stall. This study considers that process of corporate discernment and embodiment as central to the mission and worship of the church.[1]

Wells's frustration raises several important questions, and highlights the question why preaching is an appropriate practice to consider in the argument of this book. Wells highlights two common conceptions about preaching. First, preaching as a practice is about the preacher crafting words; it is a "cerebral or verbal practice" on many accounts.[2] If it is a

---

1. Wells, *Improvisation*, 18.
2. Of course, "cerebral or verbal" and embodied, social might be false alternatives.

practice, it is the practice of the preacher, a practice that the preacher allows others to observe at its climax. Second, it is often presumed that preaching is not a social practice. Wells thinks it should be, but in most cases preaching does not exhibit the embodied social discernment to be a character-transforming practice.

Wells's concern about the appropriateness of preaching as a robust ecclesial practice is one anyone schooled in MacIntyre's account of practices would have, and indeed in most accounts of Christian practices preaching does not make the list precisely for these reasons.[3] I raised these concerns in the Introduction with my description of Mt. Level's understanding and practicing of preaching in its corporate life. What I do in this chapter is offer a theological account of preaching consistent with Mt. Level's first-order practice. Preaching is indeed, and should be, an ecclesial practice, a socially embodied practice of the church in which the church performs itself as God's gathered community. Such an argument needs to be made before we can turn to how preaching as a socially embodied practice is constitutive of the church's participation in God's very life.

The account of preaching in this chapter will be given through an examination of the theology of Dietrich Bonhoeffer, especially his infrequently cited lectures on homiletics given to the students at Finkenwalde between 1935 and 1939.[4] But these lectures do not stand on their own and cannot be understood on their own. They find their place within the ecclesiological and christological themes that mark Bonhoeffer's work from the writing of *Sanctorum Communio* to his prison letters, themes that reach their fullest articulation in the very years he was giving his lectures on homiletics. When Bonhoeffer's lectures are considered within their place in his wider ecclesiology and Christology—what I call his christo-ecclesiology, because the two cannot be separated—we will see that he offers just such a robust account of preaching necessary to understand the church's practice of preaching as a socially embodied activity. Furthermore, the christological specification he gives to his understanding of the act of preaching shows preaching to be a practice by which the church is taken into the very life of God, and as such, is a practice by

---

Verbal is embodied and social and not necessarily cerebral in the negative, Cartesian sense. Wittgenstein has shown us this, too. See the discussion of embodiment in chapter 4.

3. Hütter, with his adoption of Luther's marks of the church, is an exception. See Huetter, *Suffering Divine Things*, 129.

4. Bonhoeffer, *Worldly Preaching*.

which the church relates to the world, bringing the world into its own activity and into God's. Dietrich Bonhoeffer will help me to show that when the church is practicing its own identity through preaching, Christ is practicing himself in the world, bringing the world into the church's practice, into redemption, into God's life.

BONHOEFFER'S HOMILETICS BETWEEN SCHLEIERMACHER AND TODAY

Situating Bonhoeffer's homiletics within the context established by Friedrich Schleiermacher's account of preaching in his *The Christian Faith* is important for three reasons. First, when Bonhoeffer writes about both preaching and the church he does it self-consciously with Schleiermacher in mind. Both *Sanctorum Communio* and his lectures on homiletics are scattered with quotations and allusions to Schleiermacher, most frequently as negative examples. Second, Schleiermacher's account of preaching parallels the interiorizing—and thus disappearance—of the church in modern ecclesiology. Third, Schleiermacher is a crucial figure for understanding homiletics today. Since one of the purposes of this chapter is to offer a constructive account of preaching as a corporate practice of the church, an account that stands at odds with dominant strands in homiletics, a look at one of the central figures that helped homiletics get where it is today and a glance at where it is today is not unimportant for this project.

Preaching in Schleiermacher's The Christian Faith

For Schleiermacher true piety consists in the "feeling of absolute dependence," a feeling universal to humanity. This "feeling of absolute dependence" is foundational for his dogmatic program, for in its universality it replaces any need to prove the existence of God; indeed, it presupposes God. Furthermore, this feeling of absolute dependence is an inward, prelinguistic feeling. It finds its expression in all the outward manifestations of Christianity—doctrine, ritual, preaching, etc.—but in itself the feeling of absolute dependence is a generic, undifferentiated anthropological presupposition to any and all positive religious expression. This feeling is underived and forms the essence of piety. However diverse the outward expressions of piety are, and they are as diverse as all religious expression, the inward essence of the religious feeling is identical in every instance;

it is "the consciousness of being absolutely dependent, or, that is the same thing, of being in relation with God."[5] As he says, "If the feeling of absolute dependence, expressing itself as consciousness of God, is the highest grade of immediate self-consciousness, it is also an essential element of human nature."[6]

Preaching has a direct relationship to this feeling of absolute dependence and a crucial role in bringing individuals to consciousness of it. "As regards the feeling of absolute dependence in particular, everyone will know that it was first awakened in him in the same way, by the communicative and stimulative power of expression or utterance."[7] In Christianity, that awakening is expressed as a coming to know one's need for redemption and then coming to faith in Christ, which Schleiermacher describes as the knowledge that one is no longer in the state of needing redemption. This awakening occurs through Christian preaching and principally through the preacher's rhetorical and rousing representation of his own inward experience of the same awakening. An important passage from *The Christian Faith* is worth quoting in full:

> In the same sense we spoke above of faith in God, which was nothing but the certainty concerning the feeling of absolute dependence, as such, i.e. as conditioned by a Being placed outside of us, and as expressing our relation to that Being. The faith of which we are now speaking, however, is a purely factual certainty, but a certainty of a fact which is entirely inward. That is to say, it cannot exist in an individual until, through an impression which he has received from Christ, there is found in him a beginning—perhaps quite infinitesimal, but yet a real premonition—of the process which will put an end to the state of needing redemption. . . . And so from the beginning only those people have attached themselves to Christ in His new community whose religious self-consciousness had taken the form of a need of redemption, and who now became assured in themselves of Christ's redeeming power. So that the more strongly those two phases appeared in any individual, the more able was he, by representation of the fact (which includes a description of Christ and His work) to elicit this inward experience in others. Those in whom this took place became believers, and the rest did not. *This, moreover, is what has ever since constituted the essence of*

5. Schleiermacher, *Christian Faith*, 12.
6. Ibid., 26.
7. Ibid., 27.

any direct Christian preaching. Such preaching must always take the
form of testimony; testimony as to one's own experience, which shall
arouse in others the desire to have the same experience.[8]

The transmission of faith from Christ's own preaching to the disciples through the preaching of believers in the church involves the outward representation of one's inward experience of coming to faith—the coming to consciousness of one's absolute dependence on God—to others in a way that arouses in the listener the desire to have the same experience. Thus, as he says, preaching is always the testimony *of one's own inward experience.*

In his discussion of the relationship between the outward expression of piety as preaching and the outward expression of piety as dogmatics, Schleiermacher offers a brief account of Christian preaching. Religious feeling presupposes communicability, first expressed in the immediacy of gestures and expression, but receiving in time enough cultivation to be expressed verbally. In expression, religious feeling moves from a "low development of human spirit" to a higher level. "It is only when this procedure has reached such a point of cultivation as to be able to represent itself outwardly in definite speech, that it produces real doctrine."[9] Thus doctrine for Schleiermacher is the cultivated outward expression of religious experience and so is preaching.[10] As he writes:

> The whole work of the Redeemer Himself was conditioned by the communicability of His self-consciousness by means of speech, and similarly Christianity has always and everywhere spread itself solely by preaching. Every proposition which can be an element of the Christian preaching is also a doctrine, because it bears witness to the determination of the religious self-consciousness as inward certainty. And every Christian doctrine is also a part of the Christian preaching, because every such doctrine expresses as a certainty the approximation to the state of blessedness which is to be effected through the means ordained by Christ.[11]

When, for Schleiermacher, the affective religious self-consciousness reaches a certain stage of development, it issues in utterances that are the

8. Ibid., 68–69; emphasis added.

9. Ibid., 77.

10. Thus George Lindbeck points to Schleiermacher as the beginning of what he calls the "experiential-expressive" account of doctrine. See Lindbeck, *Nature of Doctrine*, 21.

11. Schleiermacher, *Christian Faith*, 77–78.

speech-symbolic expressions of the internal religious emotion. Doctrine for Schleiermacher is the cultivated outward expression of these religious emotions; and preaching as the re-presentation of these doctrines in a rhetorical mode endeavors to elicit religious emotion, the highest of which is a feeling of dependence. Doctrines, for Schleiermacher, express and isolate in human speech the religious experience; homiletics uses human speech to rouse the very human consciousness to that religious experience that it finds codified in doctrine. Preaching is the vehicle for rousing the inward consciousness of the feeling of absolute dependence and bringing it to outward expression.[12]

Rousing Rhetoric in Homiletics Today

This way of approaching preaching is alive and well in the world of homiletical theory.[13] One of the greatest proponents of Schleiermacherian experientialism in preaching, Eugene Lowry, has not confined his speculations to his book written in 1980, *The Homiletical Plot*. There he was clear enough that he hoped the "revelatory clue" of the sermon would be "*experienced* by the congregation rather than simply known."[14] His homiletical plot is a method of sermon preparation by which to assure that such experience takes place, for if you execute it properly "there is therefore no option [for the hearer] but to stay involved in the sermonic process."[15]

In his more recent book, *The Sermon: Dancing at the Edge of Mystery*, Lowry revised his method, making it even clearer that the goal of the sermon is to evoke a certain experience. He writes, "Preaching is an offering intending to evoke an event that cannot be coerced into being."[16] For Lowry, proclamation does not occur, even though preaching might happen, if an experience is not evoked. "Preaching is our task," he writes, "Proclaiming the Word is the realized goal. Perhaps the act of evocation may become the bridge, the spanning medium of possibility, between

12. I have made this argument elsewhere in a less expanded form in the context of a conversation about the relationship between theology and rhetoric in preaching. There, too, I use Lowry and Taylor. See Owens, "Jesus Christ Is His Own Rhetoric," 187–94.

13. The finest and most thorough discussion of the influence of this kind of experiencialism in modern homiletics is Campbell, *Preaching Jesus*.

14. Lowry, *Plot*, 48; emphasis in original.

15. Ibid., 38.

16. Lowry, *Sermon*, 37.

preaching and proclaiming."[17] He then offers a modified version of his homiletical plot as a rhetorical means by which to evoke a religious experience.

An example from one of today's most prominent practitioners of preaching will illustrate the extent of the influence of Schleiermacher's notion of preaching as the evocation of religious emotion. For Barbara Brown Taylor, the interior response and experience of the individual listener is of utmost importance. In her *The Preaching Life* she writes,

> With any luck, where the sermon finally leads both preacher and congregation is into the presence of God, a place that cannot be explained but only experienced. Everyone involved in it goes away with images, thoughts, and emotions as the process of discovery goes on and on.[18]

The job of the sermon is to lead into the presence of God, and it is the preacher's effective use of words that does the leading. The presence of God, moreover, is an experience "that cannot be explained." A sermon of her's for Trinity Sunday ends:

> Meanwhile, I do not know why we hold ourselves responsible for explaining things that cannot be explained. Perhaps the most faithful sermon on the Trinity is one that sniffs around the edges of mystery, hunting for something closer to an experience than an understanding.[19]

In both Lowry and Taylor we see the living vestiges of Schleiermacher's account of preaching and its relationship to the religious emotions. In Part One I argued that the inner/outer dichotomy, prevalent in much work in ecclesiology, allows one to argue for the particularity and continuity of the church (that which is internal, invisible) at the expense of the church's human embodiment. Since interiority cannot be described in material terms, though this interiority constitutes for many the essence of the church, the concrete social processes that make up the church are not essential to the church's existence and identity. In the three figures we have briefly considered, we can see how this inner/outer dichotomy applied to the task of preaching robs us of any way of understanding the church's practice of preaching as just that, a corporate practice in the full-

17. Ibid., 38.
18. Taylor, *Preaching Life*, 83.
19. Taylor, *Home*, 154.

est sense of the word. Furthermore, this making anthropological the task of preaching also robs us of any way to understand how the church's practice of preaching implicates the church in the life of God. Insufficiently corporate and insufficiently christological, these accounts of preaching, which focus on rousing the religious emotion of the individual, make it impossible to see the church's practice of preaching as a practice of participation in the life of God and a practice by which the church practices its own identity, its own existence in the world. I turn to the work of Dietrich Bonhoeffer to offer an alternative account.

BONHOEFFER'S CHRISTO-ECCLESIOLOGY

Christo-ecclesiology in Sanctorum Communio

Bonhoeffer writes near the end of his first doctoral dissertation, *Sanctorum Communio*

> We believe that God has made the concrete, empirical church in which the word is preached and the sacraments are celebrated to be God's own church-community. We believe that it is the body of Christ, Christ's presence in the world, and that according to the promise, God's Spirit is at work in it. We have faith that God is at work in others. We do not believe in the call of individuals, but rather in that of the Church community. . . . We believe in the church as *una*, since it is "Christ existing as church-community," and *Christ is the one Lord* over those who are all one in him; as *sancta*, since the Holy Spirit is at work in it; as *catholica*, since as *God's church* its call is to the entire world, and wherever in the world God's word is preached, there is the church.[20]

In this passage written very early in his career, we already see the emergence of an ecclesiology that will last throughout his life.[21] First, we find Bonhoeffer affirming the work of the Spirit in the church. For Bonhoeffer, the actualization of the church of which Christ is the cornerstone is not a human possibility. Rather, it is the Holy Spirit who actualizes and maintains the church: "The church does not come into being by people coming together (genetic sociology), rather its existence is sustained by the Spirit

---

20. Bonhoeffer, *Sanctorum Communio*, 280; emphasis in original.

21. My understanding of Bonhoeffer's ecclesiology is influenced by Clifford Green's important *Bonhoeffer*. Consequently, my reading will highlight the development within the continuity of Bonhoeffer's christological account of the church.

who is a reality within the church community."[22] The church could not and would not exist and continue to exist and Christians could not embody Christian love without the initial and continued sustaining activity of the Spirit.[23]

Second, when Bonhoeffer writes, "We believe the church is *una* because it is 'Christ existing as church community,'" he expresses the ecclesiological insight that comprises the culminating thesis of Bonhoeffer's book and, in a way, of his career: "In and through Christ the church is established in reality. It is not as if Christ could be abstracted from the church; rather, it is none other than Christ who 'is' the church. Christ does not represent it; only what is not present can be represented. In God's eyes, however, the church is present in Christ. Christ did not merely make the church possible, but rather realized it for eternity."[24] What does Bonhoeffer mean when he says the church is "Christ existing as church-community" and "Christ 'is' the church"? The answer to this question is the heart of Bonhoeffer's christo-ecclesiology.

Sanctorum Communio gives an account of the human fall from its primal community and how that fall created the problem of human individuality, isolation, and social division. Sin, as an act of Adam, the first representative of collective humanity, destroyed the possibility of true human community.[25] Christ comes as the representative of the new humanity, the new collective person, and reestablishes the possibility of true human community lost through the fall. This possibility, actualized through the Holy Spirit, is the church.

Christ, for Bonhoeffer, is at once the founder of the church, Lord over it, but also the church itself; as Bonhoeffer writes, "Thus the church is

22. Bonhoeffer, *Sanctorum Communio*, 160. This approach to the origin of the church is clearly distinguishable from Schleiermacher, who says, "The Christian Church takes shape through the coming together of regenerate individuals to form a system of mutual interaction and cooperation" (532). Bonhoeffer summarizes his critique of Schleiermacher's ecclesiology: "In summary, we have to say that Schleiermacher not only fails to understand social community, and thus the essence of social 'unity', but that, in spite of his efforts to develop the concepts of the corporate life and the union of humanity, he does not reach the social sphere at all. It is thus just as incorrect to call him a collectivist, as it is to call him an individualist" (*Sanctorum Communio*, 193 n. 68).

23. For Bonhoeffer's argument concerning the Spirit's actualization of the church see *Sanctorum Communio*, 157–206.

24. Ibid., 157.

25. Ibid., 107–22.

already completed in Christ, just as in Christ its beginning is established. Christ is the cornerstone and the foundation of the building, and yet the church, composed of all its parts, is also Christ's body."[26] Christ's work of reconciliation brings human individuals, condemned after the fall to an unfulfilled social reality characterized by isolation, "into the church— that is, into the humanity of Christ."[27] It needs to be stressed that with Bonhoeffer, the church really is the body of Christ in a non-metaphorical way; "body" is not a trope.[28]

Working out how Bonhoeffer characterizes this relationship between Christ and the church can be tricky. It is a temptation to think that Bonhoeffer *simply* identifies Christ with the church. While this is not the case, we should not be afraid to say with Bonhoeffer that "Christ 'is' the Church" if we keep in mind appropriate qualifications. As Bonhoeffer writes,

> Paul repeatedly identifies Christ and the church community. . . . Where the body of Christ is, there Christ truly is. Christ is in the church-community, as the church-community is in Christ. . . . 'To be in Christ' is synonymous with 'to be in the church-community.' . . . Connected with this thought is the idea of the church-community as a collective personality, which again can be called Christ. . . . A complete identification between Christ and the church-community cannot be made, since Christ has ascended into heaven and is now with God, and we still await Christ's coming. This is a problem that remains unsolved.[29]

For Bonhoeffer, Christ is always over the church, its Head and Lord, creatively and freely present in the church. So the "Church 'is' Christ" only on Christ's terms, in his freedom. While the church somehow "is" Christ, the church never "has" Christ as a possession.

A helpful summary is worth quoting in full, drawing together the themes of Adam and broken community into a discussion of the church as the body of Christ. It is also helpful because it introduces another important theme—Christ as vicarious representative of the new humanity.

26. Ibid., 142.

27. Ibid., 143.

28. That "body" is not a trope is at the heart of Robert Jenson's ecclesiology. This will be discussed in chapter 5 in much greater depth.

29. Bonhoeffer, *Sanctorum Communio*, 140. Again, this issue will be taken up again in the discussion of Robert Jenson's ecclesiology in chapter 5.

In Christ humanity really is drawn into community with God, just as in Adam humanity fell. And even though in the one Adam there are many Adams, yet there is only one Christ. For Adam is "representative human being," but Christ is the Lord of his new humanity. Thus everyone becomes guilty by their own strength and fault, because they themselves are Adam; each person, however, is reconciled apart from their own strength and merit, because they themselves are not Christ. While the old humanity consists of countless isolated units—each one an Adam—that are perceived as a comprehensive unity only through each individual, the new humanity is entirely concentrated in the one single historical point, Jesus Christ, and only in Christ is it perceived as whole. For in Christ, as the foundation and the body of the building called Christ's church-community, the work of God takes place and is completed. In this work Christ has a function that sheds the clearest light on the fundamental difference between Adam and Christ, namely *the function of vicarious representative*. . . . In the old humanity the whole of humanity falls anew, so to speak, with every person who sins; in Christ, however, humanity has been brought once and for all—this is essential to *real* vicarious representative action—into community with God.[30]

These christo-ecclesial themes introduced in *Sanctorum Communio*—Christ existing as church-community, Christ as Lord over the church, and Christ as vicarious representative of the new humanity—are maintained throughout Bonhoeffer's teaching and writing career.

Christo-ecclesiology in the Christology Lectures

Bonhoeffer uses similar language to talk of Christ and the church in his lectures on Christology (1933). Here he elaborates and reworks the theme of Christ as the vicarious representative of the new humanity:

Jesus Christ is for his brethren because he stands in their place. Christ stands for his new humanity before God. But if that is so, he is the new humanity. There where mankind should stand, he stands, as representative, enabled by his *pro me* structure. He is the Church. He not only acts for it, he is it, when he goes to the cross, carries sins and dies.[31]

---

30. Bonhoeffer, *Sanctorum Communio*, 146; emphasis in original.
31. Bonhoeffer, *Christ the Center*, 48.

Bonhoeffer's articulation of the *pro nobis* structure of Christ is the most significant development in his Christology, largely present in *Sanctorum Communio* in the discussion of Christ as vicarious representative who gives himself for the church. In the Christology lectures, Bonhoeffer presents the *pro nobis* structure of Christ as an ontological description of who Christ is. Christ would not be Christ if he did not exist "for us." For Bonhoeffer, there is no such thing as Christ existing for himself. "Christ is not first a Christ for himself and then a Christ in the Church. He who alone is the Christ is the one who is present in the Church *pro me*."[32]

In the Christology lectures, Bonhoeffer identifies three forms of Christ: Christ as Word, Christ as sacrament, and Christ as church. In his discussion of "Christ as church," Bonhoeffer's christo-ecclesiology achieves its clearest expression. "Between his ascension and his coming again," Bonhoeffer writes, "the Church is his form and indeed his only form."[33] And again: "What does it mean that Christ as *Word* is also Church? It means that the Logos of God has existence in space and time in and as the Church. . . . The Church is thus not only the receiver of the Word of revelation, but is itself revelation and Word of God."[34] Again, arguing that the language of "body" is not a trope, Bonhoeffer writes, "The Church is the body of Christ. Here body is not only a symbol. The Church *is* the body of Christ, it does not *signify* the body of Christ. When applied to the Church, the concept of body is not only a concept of function, which refers only to the members of this body. It is a comprehensive and central concept of the mode of existence of the one who is present in his exaltation and humiliation."[35]

Even with this identification of Christ and the church, he does not confuse Christ with the church, for the church, even the church that *is* Word of revelation, still receives the Word of revelation and thus is never clearly and unambiguously in possession of it. He continues to maintain the freedom of Christ, who is the church, over the church, for the "Word is also itself Church, *in so far as the Church itself is revelation and the Word wishes to have the form of a created body*."[36] But we cannot allow these

32. Ibid., 47.
33. Ibid., 58.
34. Ibid., 58.
35. Ibid., 59.
36. Ibid.; emphasis added.

qualifications to diminish the thrust of Bonhoeffer's christo-ecclesiology: "Christ is not only the head of the Church, but also the Church itself." [37]

Christo-ecclesiology in Discipleship

While Bonhoeffer's earlier work on the church and Christ finds its fulfill-ment, so to speak, in these Christology lectures, they also point forward to themes in later writings. And indeed, as we turn to *Discipleship* we will notice how these christological themes are similarly expressed. What we also notice, however, is that certain themes are intensified, particularly the theme of Christ's identity with the church based on the *pro nobis* struc-ture of Christ, his vicarious giving of himself for and standing in the place of the new humanity.

When Jesus takes on flesh Jesus takes on all humanity and thus makes it the new humanity. Having taken on the weakness and sin of humanity, Jesus lives, dies, rises, and ascends on behalf of this new humanity, indeed with this new humanity in his flesh. Jesus did everything that he did "for us" so that he might constitute the new humanity, the church.[38] According to Bonhoeffer, Paul was able to express in many ways the mystery of the incarnation, but one way sums up all the rest: the *pro nobis* structure of Christ's existence. Bonhoeffer writes, "The body of Jesus Christ is 'for us' in the strictest sense of the word—on the cross, in the word, in baptism, and in the Lord's Supper. All bodily community with Jesus Christ rests on this fact."[39]

And just because the *pro nobis* structure of Chirst is the ground of all "bodily community" with Christ, Bonhoeffer can reiterate certain claims with a clarity and force found neither in *Sanctorum Communio* nor the Christology lectures:

> The body of Jesus Christ is identical with the new humanity which he has assumed. The body of Christ is his church-community [Gemeinde]. Jesus Christ at the same time is himself and his church-community (1 Cor. 12:12). Since Pentecost Jesus Christ lives here on earth in the form of his body, the church-community. Here is his body crucified and risen, here is the humanity he as-sumed. To be baptized therefore means to become a member of the church-community, a member of the body of Christ (Gal. 3:28;

37. Ibid.
38. Bonhoeffer, *Discipleship*, 213ff.
39. Ibid., 217.

1 Cor. 12:13). To be in Christ means to be in the church-community. But if we are in the church-community, then we are also truly
and bodily in Jesus Christ. This insight reveals the full richness
of meaning contained in the concept of the body of Christ. Since
the ascension, Jesus Christ's place on earth has been taken by his
body, the church [Kirche]. The church is the present Christ himself. With this statement we are recovering an insight about the
church which has been almost totally forgotten. While we are used
to thinking of the church as an institution, we ought instead to
think of it as a *person* with a body, although of course a person in
a unique sense.[40]

In this extraordinary passage we see that Bonhoeffer re-articulates an important theme of *Santorum Communio*, though without the sociological
distinctions and the necessity of explaining how the church is a collective
person as the body of Christ. Here the concept of body has been simpli-
fied: "body" means one's presence to another. Thus the presence of Christ
to the world, since the ascension, is the church; the church is his "body."

The language Bonhoeffer uses here in *Discipleship* to describe the
church becomes crucial because Christ, for Bonhoeffer, is the "new human being." "The 'new human being' is thus at the same time Christ and
the church. Christ is the new humanity in the new human being. Christ is
the church. . . . The new human being is not the single individual who has
been justified and sanctified; rather, the new human being is the church-
community, the body of Christ, or Christ himself."[41] He makes this claim
without rescinding his earlier contention that the distinction must still be
maintained between Christ and the church: "The unity between Christ
and his body, the church, demands that we at the same time recognize
Christ's lordship over his body. . . . The distinction [between head and
body] is clearly preserved; Christ is the Lord." He continues:

> The same Christ who is present in his church-community will
> return from heaven. In both cases it is the same Lord and it is the

40. Ibid., 217–18. See Sopko, "Bonhoeffer," 81–88. In that article Sopko offers a com-
parison between Bonhoeffer's and an Orthodox ecclesiology. Sopko writes, "[Bonhoeffer's]
views on the sacraments and the ministry parallel those of Orthodox ecclesiology, particularly with respect to the centrality of the Eucharist. His close identification between
Christ and the Church and his emphasis on the Church as an active agent in creating
Christ's kingdom here and now are also of the utmost importance in Orthodox ecclesiology" (88).

41. Bonhoeffer, *Discipleship*, 219.

same church; in both cases it is the very same body of the one who is present here and now, and the one who will return in the clouds. However, it makes serious difference whether we are here or there. Thus, both the unity and the distinction are necessary aspects of the same truth.[42]

Here in *Discipleship*, then, we see clearly—perhaps most clearly—the important ecclesial themes present in both *Sanctorum Communio* and the Christology lectures.

In this book I am arguing that the church should be understood as Christ practicing himself in the Spirit for the sake of the world. While I will continue to argue for this way of speaking as the book progresses, what I want to note now is that Bonhoeffer's ecclesiology begins to lay the foundation, so to speak, to make sense of that language. An ecclesiology like his, which points to the way the church as a body can be understood to be Christ himself precisely because of Christ's *pro nobis* structure, offers the conceptual tools to make sense of my saying that the church is Christ practicing himself in the Spirit. By using the language of "Christ practicing himself in the Spirit," I want to show both the embodied and Trinitarian aspects of the church's participation in God, both largely ignored in ecclesiology more generally, as the first chapter showed, and to show how through embodied practices of the church, God is taking the church into his own active life of Father, Son, and Holy Spirit.

But a fully *trinitarian* understanding of the church needs attention to pneumatology. Bonhoeffer's ecclesiology in *Discipleship* is helpful here as well, for his pneumatology helps to keep him from collapsing any distinction between Christ and the church and also maintain that the life of the church is the life of God. Another passage is worth quoting at length:

> The unity of the church-community gives identity and meaning to each individual and to the community as a whole, just as Christ and his body give identity and meaning to the church-community. It is at this point that the office of the Holy Spirit is thrown into sharp relief. It is the Holy Spirit who brings Christ to the individuals (Eph. 3:17, 1 Cor. 12:3). It is the Spirit who builds up the church by gathering individuals, even though in Christ the whole building is already complete (Eph. 2:22, 4:12, Col. 2:7). The Holy Spirit creates the community (2 Cor. 13:13) of the members of the body (Rom. 15:30; 5:5; Col. 1:8; Eph. 4:3). The Lord is the Spirit (2 Cor. 3:17).

42. Ibid., 220.

> The church of Christ is Christ present through the Holy Spirit. The
> life of the body of Christ has thus become our life. In Christ we no
> longer live our own lives, but Christ lives his life in us. The life of
> believers in the church-community is truly *the life of Jesus Christ in
> them* (Gal. 2:20, Rom. 8:10, 2 Cor. 13:5; 1 John 4:15).[43]

The church, as the body of Christ, lives its life by the Holy Spirit. This
is what Bonhoeffer means in *Sanctorum Communio* when he says the
Spirit "actualizes the church."[44] The church, when it performs its own
identity through its distinctive practices, is indeed living the life of God,
participating in the life of God, precisely through its christological and
pneumatological dimensions. A fuller trinitarian account of participation will require further pneumatological specification, which I will offer
in chapter 6. Here it is only necessary to say that in Bonhoeffer, we see
the beginning theological rational for an account of the church as Christ
himself, qualified appropriately pneumatologically, living the life of God,
that is, participating in God's active life.

One final point before turning to Bonhoeffer's positive account of
preaching: the church's life in God is a visible, embodied life. "The Body
of Christ," Bonhoeffer expresses bluntly, "takes up physical space here
on earth. By becoming human Christ claims a place among us human
beings. He came unto his own. . . . [T]he incarnation does entail the
claim to space granted on earth, and anything that takes up space is
visible. Thus the body of Jesus Christ can only be a visible body, or else
it is not a body at all. . . . The body of the exalted Lord is likewise a
visible body, taking the form of the church-community."[45] Bonhoeffer
here is making clear that none of the language of participation, none
of the language of the church as Christ made possible by the Spirit, is
abstract. The very church that is the body of Christ, precisely because
it is a body, is *visible*; moreover, it is visible through its practices. "How
does the body become visible?" he writes. "First in the *preaching of the
word*."[46] As we will see, the church's practice of preaching is one of the
chief ways for Bonhoeffer in which the church performs its visibility.

43. Ibid., 221; emphasis in original.

44. Bonhoeffer, *Sanctorum Communio*, 157ff.

45. Bonhoeffer, *Discipleship*, 225–26. This emphasis on the visibility of the church as
the form of Christ stands as an alternative to the traditional dichotomies (visible/invis-
ible, inner/outer) that were critiqued in the previous chapter.

46. Ibid., 226; emphasis in original.

The embodied visibility of the church is not a static embodiment, in the same way that a dead body is no longer a human body. Rather, the church practices its embodiment, and in that practicing the body itself is visible. The church, through proclamation and other practices, takes up space in the world. "That the community of Jesus Christ claims a *space* in this world *for its proclamation* is now clear."[47] The space for that proclamation is precisely the visible space the church takes up as it practices itself in its proclamation of Christ, who is the body's space.

Before turning to Bonhoeffer's account of the church's ministry of preaching, let me summarize the five christo-ecclesial themes in his writing. First, Christ exists in and as the church; the church is really the Body of Christ, Christ's visible present in the world, in time and space, and thus Christ's availability to the world. Second, Christ's existing as the church is possible because of Chirst's *pro nobis* structure. Christ cannot exist other than "for us," as the collective person, the representative of the new humanity who is himself the new humanity who stands in place of the new humanity, redeems the new humanity, and makes the church the body of the new humanity. Christ is always existing "for us" or Christ is not Christ. Third, while Christ is the church, the identity of Christ and the Church cannot be simply collapsed, for Christ remains Lord and Head of the church, ever calling it to follow obediently. Fourth, this distinction between Christ and the church is given briefly pneumatologically. Though it will need to be filled out, that the church is Christ has already been specified by Bonhoeffer pneumatologically. Finally, the church takes up space in the world; as the body of Christ, it has a peculiar form into which it is always being transformed, and that form is the form of Christ himself.

For Bonhoeffer the visibility of the church as Christ's body in the world depends to a large degree on the church's ministry of preaching. The community of Christ, or Christ existing in the world as the church community, takes up space and time, Bonhoeffer claims, and thus must be a visible body. "How does it become visible? First in the preaching of the Word."[48]

47. Ibid., 229; emphasis in original.
48. Ibid., 226.

BONHOEFFER ON PREACHING AS A PRACTICE
OF PARTICIPATION IN GOD

I hope it is clear how he talks about the church in terms of participation. As Christ, as Christ's body, as that body which lives Christ's life in the world through the Spirit, the church is humanity's embodied participation in the triune God. The dependence of his ecclesiology on a strong, one could say Alexandrian, reading of Chalcedon establishes his claim that Christ is the church insofar as the church is the new humanity assumed by Christ as Christ's own humanity. "Christ 'is' the Church" is, with appropriate qualifications, the foundation of Bonhoeffer's ecclesiology. It is also his christological account of participation. What we need to see now is how through the practice of preaching the church is enacting this participation in Christ; or, to put it differently, how the church's practicing itself *is* God's sharing his life with the church; or, to put it differently again, how in the church's practice of proclamation Christ is practicing himself in the Spirit.

Proclamation as a Practice of the Church

When considering the MacIntyrean description of practices, one is not likely to think immediately of preaching. In what way is preaching a cooperative human activity that extends over time? Doesn't preaching usually seem to be the activity of a particular individual, fulfilling a task while the congregation sits passively by, usually bored? What are the goods of preaching and how are they intrinsic to the activity itself? Remember, for Schleiermacher and for the homiletics inspired by him, preaching is not a cooperative human activity, but the preacher's own witness to his or her own inward experience for the purpose of eliciting that same experience in others. Logically, then, preaching is prior to the church and not an activity of the church itself. Furthermore, the ends of preaching are not intrinsic to preaching, but preaching is a means to an extrinsic end. Proclamation, as Lowry said, has not occurred unless the desired internal effect has been produced in the hearer. Preaching's purpose is to rouse in the listener humanity's innate sense of dependence on God. Preaching is related to this as a means to an end, but it is not an end in itself. But if preaching has no internal goods intrinsic to the activity itself, and is related to the rousing of religious emotion as a means to an end, then is not preaching dispensable if another, more effective, means of rousing the religious emotion is discovered? This dominant account of preaching in modernity leaves little room to see how preaching itself can be an embodied, corporate activity; even less, how preaching is an activity of the church, through which the church practices its identity in the world as Christ's body.

To the question of whether preaching will ever be dispensable Bonhoeffer must answer an emphatic, "No!" All these might be possible if it had not been the Word of God who assumed a new humanity. Any notion that the preaching of the Word is dispensable is a *denial that God is the God who sent his Word to become flesh*. Or, to put it differently, to affirm the dispensability of the preached word is to deny the triunity of God. The mission of the church to preach the word is not incidental to the kind of God the church has, precisely because the mission of the church is an extension of the mission of the Son, the incarnate Logos of the Father, as the church is that Son's body in the world. Here is how Bonhoeffer describes the relations of the preached Word to the mission of the second Person of the Trinity in *Discipleship*:

> They [the apostles] have seen the Word of God with their own eyes, how it had come into the world and assumed human flesh, and with it the whole human race. Now they were compelled to bear witness to nothing else but the fact that God's Word had become flesh, and had come to accept sinners, to forgive their sins and sanctify them. *It is the same Word which now enters the church-community.* The Word made flesh, the Word which already bears the whole human race, the Word which can no longer exist in isolation from the humanity it has assumed—this same Word now comes to the church-community. And in this Word comes the Holy Spirit, revealing to the single individual and to the church-community the gifts they have already been given in Jesus Christ. The Holy Spirit bestows faith on the hearers, enabling them to believe that, in the word of preaching Jesus Christ himself has come to be present in our midst in the power of his body.[49]

That last line is crucial to understand the intrinsic goods of preaching: "[I]n the word of preaching Jesus Christ himself has come to be present in our midst in the power of his body." That coming is intrinsic to the act of preaching itself and is not an external good, like the rousing of religious emotion, which only happens with the preachers artful use

49. Ibid., 228; emphasis in original.

of rhetoric.[50] Under those circumstances, the result of preaching is not intrinsic to the activity itself. Another way of putting the matter, as I have argued elsewhere,[51] is that for Bonhoeffer, Jesus Christ is his own rhetoric. In most speeches "human words communicate something else besides what they are of themselves. They become a means to an end," writes Bonhoeffer.[52] When we have appropriately qualified any language of human excellence in regard to preaching, we can see rightly that preaching does have internal goods, intrinsic to the practice itself, though goods, ironically, which we cannot strive to achieve. "The meaning of the proclaimed word," Bonhoeffer writes, "does not lie outside of itself; it is the thing itself. It does not transmit anything else, it does not express anything else, it has no external objectives—rather, it communicates that it is itself: the historical Jesus Christ, who bears humanity upon himself with all its sorrows and guilt."[53] There is not a goal, a good, external to the preaching of the word that can be achieved by another means; the practice of the preaching of the word is itself the incarnate Word of God bearing humanity. And there are no further goals to the preaching of the word—comfort, encouragement, motivation—that are not included in the word's bearing our human guilt and sorrows.

That the goods of preaching are internal to the activity itself still does not answer the question of why proclamation is not a practice of the preacher, rather than of the church, or why proclamation is considered a practice at all, and not just another activity. The answer lies in the fully ecclesial nature of the church's preaching and its relation to another practice of the church, ordination. The church is the source and goal of preaching. "I preach," he writes, "because the church is there—and I preach that the church might be there. Church preaches to church."[54] Every possible goal

50. As Frits de Lange says, "Just as salvation is present and sealed in the tangible and visible sacrament, so it is also concretely present in the audible word. The word of salvation makes salvation present. It is not a means to something else. It has no other goal than its own presence" (de Lange, *Waiting for the Word*, 95).

51. See Owens, "Jesus Christ," 192–94.

52. Bonhoeffer, *Worldly Preaching*, 103.

53. Ibid.

54. Ibid., 112. Wesley Avram in "The Work of Conscience in Bonhoeffer's Homiletic," nicely summarizes the point: "Preaching is [for Bonhoeffer], to put it crassly, the vocal chords of Christ's spiritual body. It is significant and irreplaceable less by its content than by its very happening" (6). Throughout the article Avrum argues that the church's preaching to itself is analogous to the work of conscience.

of preaching—to persuade, to move, to convert, to comfort—is subsumed under this one goal that is the Word's own goal: to establish the church as the new humanity of Christ. Thus, he writes, likely with Schleiermacher in mind,

> The source of the preached word is not the pious Christian experience or the consciousness of the preacher, nor the need of the hour of the congregation, nor the desire to improve and influence others. All these things quickly collapse and lead to resignation. These motivations and forces are not enough. The only valid source of the sermon is the commission of Christ to proclaim the gospel, and also the knowledge that this commission comes to us from an already existing church. The source of the sermon is nothing other than the existence of the church of Christ.[55]

That the "source of the sermon is nothing other than the existence of the church" and that the commission to preach "comes to us from an already existing church" places preaching firmly in its ecclesial context. Unlike for Schleiermacher, for whom preaching to rouse the religious emotion is logically prior to the church, for Bonhoeffer the two are inseparable, even if the church itself has a logical priority.

This logical priority of the church—that is, the source of the preaching ministry within the church—is clear for Bonhoeffer through an account of ordination. It is the church who commissions one to preach so that the church can be the "servant of the preached word."[56] The practice of proclamation is related integrally to other activities of the church including ordination. He writes:

> The ministry of preaching constitutes the church's ministry rather than the office of the pastor. The ministry of preaching is intrinsic and remains as such; the office of pastor is a specialized division of the preaching ministry. It may be taken from us. Its form should be adapted to the preaching ministry. Ordination is the call to a preaching ministry and not primarily to the office of pastor. . . . Ordination is the conveyance of the ministry of preaching by the church in general, while the installation into a specific pastoral office is a particular act. . . . The ministry of preaching is no independent trade.[57]

55. Bonhoeffer, *Worldly Preaching*, 111.
56. Ibid., 109.
57. Ibid., 108–9.

That a trade is not independent is necessary for it to be a corporately shared and embodied practice. That this particular practice is the *church's* trade makes it a properly *ecclesial* practice.

In the face of modern accounts of preaching, which focus on the experience of the preacher and the interior response of the listener, it has been hard to see how preaching is a social practice, let alone a social practice of the church. Aimed as it has been at a goal beyond itself and the particular nature of that goal—the rousing of the religious emotions—the modern accounts of preaching from Schleiermacher to the present have tended to ignore the visible, corporate nature of the church and the essential link between the ministry of preaching and that corporate church. Bonhoeffer, by denying the existence of a goal of preaching external to the preaching of the Word itself, and by locating preaching as a ministry of the church made possible by the practice of ordination, has shown that preaching is indeed a practice of the church and not an isolated independent trade, thus giving us the resources to recover a robust account of preaching as an embodied practice of the church by which the church practices its own identity as Christ's body.

Proclamation as Christological Participation in the Life of God

If the preaching ministry of the church is a fully corporate practice, finding its source, goal, and intelligibility in the church, how for Bonhoeffer does this very practice constitute, among other practices, the church's participation in the life of God? The argument follows directly from Bonhoeffer's christo-ecclesiology. The church is the embodied Christ; its life is Christ's life; and its form is the form of Christ.

Since the church itself is the new humanity assumed by Christ, then to show how proclamation is christological participation in the life of God, Bonhoeffer needs to make only one more move, which he does when he argues, "The proclaimed word *is the Christ bearing human nature.*"[58] This must be true if the word proclaimed is indeed the Logos of God, for on the principle of Chalcedon (the enhypostatic/anhypostatic union), after the incarnation there is no Logos without humanity just as there is no human Jesus without the Logos. So, "the proclaimed word is the Christ bearing human nature." This very point he clarifies, using the strongest participation language: "This is no new incarnation, but the Incarnate

58. Ibid., 102; emphasis in original.

One who bears the sins of the world. Through the Holy Spirit the word becomes the actualization of his acceptance and sustenance. Because the Word includes us into himself, it makes us into the body of Christ." Proclamation is participation in the life of God precisely because the proclaimed word is the Logos of God who "includes us into himself" through the Holy Spirit. A few paragraphs later he puts it a little differently: "As the Logos has adopted human nature, so the spoken word actualizes our adoption."[59] Preaching itself is participation in the life of God. When the church practices proclamation, the church, as the body of Christ, is practicing its own identity as the new humanity. As the embodied church and the flesh of Christ, the church, in its preaching, participates in the life of God so as to say that the church itself, in its activity of preaching, embodies its participation in God's own active life as Trinity.

But before turning to an account of this participation's visibility, there is another passage we need to consider, for it sets the limits, so to speak, of christological participation. While it initially sounds like Bonhoeffer is denying participation in any robust sense, he is only saying what the Christian tradition has always maintained needs to be said when talking of participation. Even when the church uses the language of deification, it must make clear that we never become divine so as to be not-created. Bonhoeffer is guarding against a latent eutychianism that is like the shade at the church's right hand whenever it talks about deification.[60] He is ruling out this error when he writes, "While the Word accepts and sustains us, there is nevertheless no fusion of God's being with ours, no identification of the godly nature with the human nature. . . . There is no mystical metamorphosis that occurs, but rather faith and sanctification."[61] This language—"fusion," "identification," "metamorphosis"—shows Bonhoeffer's attentiveness to the issues of Chalcedon. He is not denying the notion of participation, but setting the parameters, so to speak, for faithful Christian talk of participation, speech that respects the limits set on the church's speech at the Council of Chalcedon. Within these parameters, we have the space to say quite faithfully, "the Word [in this case the preached word] includes us into itself." The practice of proclamation is God's

---

59. Ibid., 103.

60. As we saw in the introduction, some of Charles Wesley's hymns approach this very danger. In chapter 6 I will offer a much fuller account of deification in the discussion of Maximus the Confessor.

61. Bonhoeffer, *Worldly Preaching*, 104.

drawing us into the active life of God's trinity. As Bonhoeffer says, "In the proclaimed word Christ is alive as the Word of the Father. In the proclaimed word he receives the congregation into himself."[62]

For Bonhoeffer, the church as the body of Christ is Christ in the world; the church lives by the life of Christ, and indeed is the form Christ takes in the world. Christ is the church, according to Bonhoeffer. As I want to argue that through the church's embodied practices Christ practices himself in the world—the church practices its embodiment of Christ in the world—Bonhoeffer's recovery of the ancient claim that the church is a person is crucial to this argument. Though he makes appropriate distinctions between Christ and the church—for instance, that Christ is at once the church and the head of the church—this does not blunt the force of the claim, which Bonhoeffer rightly thinks is mandated by Scripture.

But how does that embodiment take place? How does the church *live* as the body of Christ, Christ's visible presence in the world? This book is arguing that the embodied social practices of the church are the church's participation in the life of God. Bonhoeffer is useful in helping to make this claim precisely, as we have seen, because his christological account of the church—Christ is the church and head of the church—is also a deeply christological account of participation. For his understanding of how the church participates in God Bonhoeffer is not dependent on philosophical ontologies,[63] but rather on what the ancient definition of Chalcedon will allow him to say. And that definition allows him to say that in the church itself is Christ's adoption of humanity, without any confusion between the divinity and the humanity. Therefore, now with the appropriate limits placed on our speech by Chalcedon, we can make more sense of my central claims in this book: 1) that in its embodied, social practices the church practices its own identity as the body of Christ in the world, which amounts to the claim 2) that the church is Christ practicing himself in the Spirit on behalf of the world, and; 3) that these embodied practices—the church's practicing its identity as Christ's body, or Christ practicing himself in the Spirit—*are*, precisely because of their christological moorings, the church's participation in the life of God.

The church's ministry of preaching is just such an embodied, social practice. Bonhoeffer gives us enough to see that preaching is a practice of

62. Ibid., 103.

63. To what extent other accounts of participation are dependent on philosophical ontologies will be discussed in chapter 5.

the church, counter to the claims of Schleiermacher and certain strands of contemporary homiletics. In its preaching, "church preaches to church." Thus I have been arguing that the practice of preaching is a particular instantiation, or embodiment, of the more general ecclesiological and christological claims. It does no good to make theological claims about the church if those claims cannot be shown to be coherent in terms of the particularities of specific practices. I have used Bonhoeffer to begin to show how preaching is just such a practice in which the church practices its identity as the body of Christ, and thus practices, in a visible and embodied way, its participation in the life of God.

Proclamation and the Shape of Participation

What does it mean to say that this practice of preaching is the church's *visible* participation in the life of God. What do I mean when I talk about the "shape of participation"?

When all of the talk of participation begins to sound very abstract, we must remember that Bonhoeffer is giving these lectures as he is writing *Discipleship* and *Life Together*, living in an illegal, underground seminary, hidden from the Nazi's penetrating gaze. We cannot think that he is dabbling in christological speculation because he has the luxury of time to engage in what must seem to some an essentially elitist activity. No, (and here again I push beyond Bonhoeffer's formulation to make one of the central claims of this book): *the gift of participation, which the church practices as Christ practices himself in the church's proclamation, has a particular shape, a form; it has its own peculiar visibility because it is the Jesus Christ of the Gospels who is practicing himself in the practices of the church.* We have already noted where Bonhoeffer gives theological arguments that support this claim. He argued,

> The church-community has, therefore, a very real impact on the life of the world. *It gains space for Christ.* . . . All who belong to the body of Christ have been freed from and called out of the world. They must become visible to the world not only through the communal bond evident in the church-community's order and worship, but also through the new communal life among brothers and sisters in Christ.[64]

64. Bonhoeffer, *Discipleship*, 236; emphasis in original.

But this claim only follows from an earlier one: "That the community of Jesus Christ claims a *space* in this world *for its proclamation* is now clear. The body of Christ becomes visible in the church-community that gathers around word and sacrament."[65] And I would push a little what Bonhoeffer says: It's not just that the church claims space for proclamation, but if proclamation is indeed what he has said it is, the very activity of proclamation itself *is* the claiming of space; it is the visibility of the church.

In the lectures on homiletics, Bonhoeffer gives further specification to these claims. Remarking that "word and deed were a unity in the life of Christ," Bonhoeffer says that "to the preaching of the word belongs the acting of the church."[66] And again, "The witness of the church involves preacher and listener in word and deed." That the proclaimed word is the Logos of God assuming the new humanity is not an empty abstraction, because it is talking about Jesus Christ. Participation has a particular shape, and his name is Jesus. Again I quote a central passage: "The meaning of the proclaimed word, however, does not lie outside of itself; it is the thing itself. It does not transmit anything else, it does not express anything else, it has no external objectives—rather, it communicates that it is itself: *the historical Jesus Christ*, who bears humanity upon himself with all its sorrows and its guilt."[67] The shape of the preaching of the word is no less visible than was the historical Jesus Christ; neither, then, is the church's participation in God.

Bonhoeffer, commenting in a way that is remarkably similar to George Lindbeck's cultural-linguistic account of truth, says:

> This causality and finality (both basically identical in significance) signified that the church preaches only *one* sermon in all its messages, and this sermon is not dependent upon current events and their circumstances. It is the *one* truth to which the church testifies. This truth is not a result of deductions; it is not the communication of a certain body of doctrine. It is truth that has taken place. It creates its own form of existence. It is possible for the church to preach pure doctrine that is nonetheless untrue. The truthfulness

65. Ibid., 229; emphasis in original.

66. Bonhoeffer, *Worldly Preaching*. Again Avram: "Only God's word can again overwhelm this power differential and restore unity. It does so in Christ, in whom the originary word is again spoken. There is no gap in Christ between word and deed, and so in him language is redeemed and words once again become deeds—spoken to and for all creation" ("Conscience," 6).

67. Bonhoeffer, *Worldly Preaching*, 103.

of it hinges upon the form of manifestation that the church adopts for itself. This form, however, implies discipleship and not proximity to what people expect or unity with their culture.[68]

Bonhoeffer's Chalcedonian account of Christianity hits the ground, so to speak, in this statement, which can only be read as a critique of the culturally accommodated Christianity of Nazi Germany. The Logos-assuming humanity cannot be abstracted from the narratives of the Gospels, where that same Logos calls people to follow in a costly way. It must be remembered: the arguments that precipitated Chalcedon were arguments about how to read the unity of Christ in the narratives of the Gospels.[69] The accommodated Christianity of Bonhoeffer's day might have maintained the "true" doctrines of Christianity, but truth for Bonhoeffer is not, in this case, getting the words right, but it is the very form that participation takes when it is participation in the Christ who cannot be abstracted from the calling-to-discipleship Christ of the Gospels. In other words, truth is visible. Critiquing again the accommodated, indeed apostate, Christianity of his day, Bonhoeffer writes, "The basis of the preaching church is not flesh and blood, customs and cultures, and its form is not one of cultural unity, but rather its basis is the Word and the from is obedience." The shape of participation is obedience. In a striking line, which must ring as a wake-up call to the culturally accommodated Christianity of our own day, Bonhoeffer writes, "The contemporary truth of the church is revealed in that it preaches and lives the Sermon on the Mount and the admonitions of Paul."[70]

At the end of all of Bonhoeffer's ecclesiological and christological reflections, along with his rich theology of preaching, lies this conclusion: the shape of participation, the shape of Christ practicing himself in the

---

68. Ibid., 113. Compare this to Lindbeck, *Nature of Doctrine*, 63–66. It is an interesting question how for Bonhoeffer one can account for failed preaching. Since preaching's instrumentality is ruled out for Bonhoeffer, it seems there is no way to account for failed preaching. Surely, for Bonhoeffer, one cannot talk narrowly about one preaching act or one sermon and judge whether it is has succeeded or failed. In fact, to ask whether preaching has succeeded or failed might be a category error. What are the implications of this for teaching preaching? I don't know.

69. Bonhoeffer himself notes that in this controversy, "The monophysites were dominated by a greater seriousness; the Nestorians, by a greater adherence to the Bible" (*Christ the Center*, 86).

70. Bonhoeffer, *Worldly Preaching*, 113.

practices of the church, is the love of enemies. The best picture of participation is the peaceable obedience of Jesus.

CONCLUSION

Phil Kenneson has argued that in Protestant theology the church as a visible community disappears with Schleiermacher.[71] This disappearance I have argued is not only evident in Schleiermacher's account of preaching, focused as it is on interiority, but also in certain dominant strands in homiletics today. Where is the church when preaching takes place? In the individual experience, many would answer. But Bonhoeffer shows us a better way, because he shows a visible, embodied church, visible especially in its ministry of proclamation. In giving us back a visible church, Bonhoeffer has given us a robust account of the church's preaching worthy of the historical Christ whom the church proclaims.

But more importantly, Bonhoeffer has helped us see more clearly how the church itself lives its life in God. While needing a more fulsome pneumatology, Bonhoeffer's christological account of the church as living God's life as the body of Christ makes substantial progress toward showing that precisely as a body, as a visible community in the world, the church's participation in God's life is also visible and embodied. The church does not reflect the life of God in its practices, nor does it join God's activity somewhere else. The church *is* God's activity (said with all the qualifications of Chalcedon in mind) as the body of Christ, practicing the life of God as it practices its own life in the world. Thus Bonhoeffer points us in the direction of answers to questions raised in the Introduction.

Furthermore, such activites take place through particular practices, especially preaching. Preaching is not an "independent trade" but is a practice of the church, and it is a practice of the church through which God brings the church into God's own life.

But more importantly, this bringing of the church into God's own life, this participation is visible, it is embodied. *The gift of participation, which the church practices as Christ practices himself in the church's proclamation, has a particular shape, a form; it has its own peculiar visibility because it is the Jesus Christ of the Gospels who is practicing himself in the*

---

71. Kenneson, "Reappearance," 108–56.

practices of the church. Bonhoeffer's account of the church and its preaching gives a glimpse of this reality.

4

Eucharist as a Practice of Participation

Herbert McCabe's Theology of the Eucharist

IN THE PREVIOUS CHAPTER on the practice of preaching, I offered a christological account of proclamation to show that preaching is both a properly ecclesial practice, an *embodied* ecclesial practice, while at the same time it is a practice of participation, which amounts to the same thing. I argued that in the practice of proclamation, Christ, as the church that is the body of Christ, is practicing his own identity even while he is the church's head and Lord. Preaching, as we saw for Bonhoeffer, is part of the church's shape, the form of its obedience; it is also the church's christological participation in the life of God. Bonhoeffer gives us an account of an ecclesial practice, articulated as participation in a particularly christological way, which cannot escape the particularity of the shape of the life of Jesus Christ as Christ continues to practice that life in the church. Thus the account of participation that I am attributing to him has a definite shape, and that shape looks for Bonhoeffer like the Sermon on the Mount and the life of Jesus. This is so because, in the same way that word and deed were a unity in the life of Christ, so word and deed are united in the life of the church. To the practice of preaching belongs organically the faithful shape of the church's existence. And this follows, not because preaching impels or motivates the church to faithfulness, but because of the theological argument that Jesus as the incarnate Logos is the embodied word and deed of God.

Here I turn to a second church-constitutive practice—the church's practice of eating together in the Eucharist. In the same way that the account of preaching was offered through the thought of a particular theologian, so too will be the discussion of the Eucharist. While his language is different from Bonhoeffer's, Herbert McCabe, OP, shows us, in the terms of the Eucharist as language, that participation in the life of God has a particular shape and a peculiar visibility.

The leap from Bonhoeffer, a German Lutheran, to McCabe, an English Dominican, might seem artificial. In reality, it is not a leap but a progression, for even if their theological contexts are extremely different, their concerns and material claims are not. Deeply influenced by his travels to Rome and his contact with Catholicism, Bonhoeffer articulates in his theology of preaching a very sacramental account of preaching, whereby the activity itself, as we have seen, is Christ's accepting humanity into God's life. Furthermore, as we saw, Bonhoeffer's account of preaching depends on Chalcedonian orthodoxy in order to make his claims. We will see that, similarly for McCabe, christological orthodoxy is crucial for understanding participation. Third, we saw with Bonhoeffer that his theology of preaching attempts to provide an alternative to those accounts stemming from Schleiermacher that are based on a sharp distinction between interiority and exteriority, between the invisible and the visible. Bonhoeffer's dismissal of the invisible church is based on his understanding that this distinction is theologically unhelpful and damaging of the church's faithfulness. That participation has a particular shape and a peculiar visibility is a direct result of his abandonment of this dualistic anthropology. Similarly, as we shall see, McCabe's account of participation is predicated on his explicit denial of what he calls a mistaken account of the relationship between mind and body, interiority and exteriority. Finally, and perhaps most importantly, Bonhoeffer's account of the shape of the church's faithfulness based on the theological point that in Christ word and deed were a unity provides an important link to McCabe's account of language and communication, which allows McCabe to say that our bodies are intrinsically communicative and that Jesus, in his body, the Eucharist, is the communication of the Father and the future in the present. While the point of using Bonhoeffer and McCabe is in no way to compare and contrast, it is important to show that the move from Bonhoeffer to McCabe is neither incoherent nor incongruent, but oddly natural.

Eucharistic practice is one of the visible, material, embodied human practices that make up the church, one of those in the web of variously enumerated practices that constitute the church. Human bodies are gathered around an altar; they feel and smell and taste the bread and wine as they chew it in their mouths. They stand, and kneel, and walk, and bow. Herbert McCabe takes this embodied nature of eucharistic practice, indeed of all ecclesial practices, as crucial as he gives us a way to talk about the Eucharist as more than a "spiritual" practice, but one that forms real human bodies into the body of Christ, and thus about how through eucharistic practice the church participates christologically in the life of God.

In this chapter I argue that McCabe helpfully shows us what participation in God is by transforming the traditional language of participation into the language of communication, so that when we participate, through the incarnation and the Eucharist, in the Word of the Father, we are participating in God's own self-communication. But that self-communication is nothing other than God's own understanding of himself through the eternal Word; that is, to share in God's self-communication is to share in the life of God's triunity. As McCabe writes, "The word of God is the way in which the Father sees himself, his realization of himself; the incarnation means that this divine self-realisation is shared with us. We are able to enter into the language, and hence the life, of the Father."[1]

LUMEN GENTIUM AND THE CHURCH AS SACRAMENT

In the same way that I situated Bonhoeffer in the history of homiletics beginning with Schleiermacher, here I want to situate McCabe within the context of twentieth-century Roman Catholic ecclesiology. First, by showing the similarities of McCabe's approach to the sacramental ecclesiology made dominant by Vatican II, we will better see the innovative aspect of McCabe's own sacramental ecclesiology. Second, it will help us relate McCabe's approach to the Eucharist and the church to the questions raised in chapter 2, especially questions about the relationship between the so-called inner/outer and theological/sociological aspects of the church. This section has three parts. First, we will look briefly at *Lumen Gentium*, which many see as the triumph of a sacramental ecclesiology over institutional/juridical approaches to the church. Second, we will look at the story Avery Dulles tells about Roman Catholic ecclesiology in his *Models of the Church*. His book has achieved nearly canonical status as an introduction to ecclesiology. By examining the story he tells of ecclesiology, then, we will better be able to see how the dominant narrative maintains the problematic distinction between the inner and outer aspects of the church and the supposed conflict between the institutional/sociological structures of the church and its theological/spiritual essence. Then, we

1. McCabe, *Law, Love, and Language*, 126.

will be in a place to see how McCabe's early discussions of the church as constituted by the sacraments both uses and subverts the language of this dominant narrative.

Lumen Gentium's *Sacramental Ecclesiology*

The first article of *Lumen Gentium* spells out the key themes addressed by the dogmatic constitution:

> Since the church is in Christ like a sacrament [*Cum autem Ecclesia sit in Christo veluti sacramentum*] or as a sign and instrument both of a very closely knit union with God and of the unity of the whole human race, it [the synod] desires now to unfold more fully to the faithful of the Church and to the whole world its own inner nature and universal mission.[2]

The first thing that must be noted is the intimate connection shown here between ecclesiology and Christology. Chapter 1 of *Lumen Gentium* spells out in detail the fully trinitarian aspects of the church, noting that from the beginning, the "eternal Father . . . had a plan to raise men to a participation in the divine life."[3] That participation, the fulfillment of the plan of the Father, is achieved by his sending the Son (Article 3) and the Spirit (Article 4) whose job it is to "continually sanctify the Church" so that "all those who believe would have access through Christ in one Spirit to the Father."[4] Nonetheless, the christological center is introduced in Article 1 and dominates the dogmatic constitution. Second, the language of the church as a sacrament is given prominent place. This is important because is expresses the constitutive relationship between the church and the sacraments, which the constitution elaborates more fully in chapter 2, "The People of God," so that it is clear that every aspect of the church's life expresses this sacramental reality. Finally, we see that the Constitution deals with the "inner nature" or essence of the church. This is important because, as I showed in chapter 1, this is the very language critiqued by Gustafson and Healy.

The first chapter of *Lumen Gentium* addresses themes important to this book, and, as we will see, to the work of McCabe. Chapter 1 is a theological argument for the unity of the church with God, taking up aspects

2. *Lumen Gentium* 1, 123.
3. *Lumen Gentium* 1.2, 124.
4. *Lumen Gentium* 1.4, 125.

of the "mystical body" ecclesiology popular in Roman Catholic theology of the late-nineteenth and early-twentieth centuries:

> In the human nature united to himself, the Son of God, by over-coming death through his own death and resurrection, redeemed and remolded him into a new creation (cf. Gal 6:15; 2 Cor 5:17). By communicating his Spirit, Christ made his brothers, called together from all nations, mystically the components of his own body. In that body the life of Christ is poured into the believers who, through the sacraments, are united in a hidden and real way to Christ who suffered and was glorified.[5]

One of the important things the Constitution does is to correct certain deficiencies in the "mystical body" ecclesiology by connecting the visible, social nature of the church with a theology of the church as united to God through a mystical union with Christ's Body:

> Christ, the one Mediator, established and continually sustains here on earth his holy Church, the community of faith, hope and char-ity, as an entity with visible delineation through which he com-municates truth and grace to all. But the society structured with hierarchical organs and the Mystical Body of Christ are not to be considered as two realities, nor are the visible assembly and the spiritual community, nor the earthly Church and the Church en-riched with heavenly things; rather they form one complex reality which coalesces from a divine and a human element.[6]

Avery Dulles's Models of the Church

In the first three chapters of his extraordinarily popular book *Models of the Church*, Avery Dulles narrates a story of the relationship among three different approaches to the church. He talks about the church as an Institution, Mystical Body, and Sacrament. These three aspects of the church are discussed in the prologue and first chapter of *Lumen Gentium*. Dulles discusses Mystical Body ecclesiology as a response to Institutional ecclesiology, and he suggests that sacramental ecclesiology brings the other two together in a synthesis.

---

5. *Lumen Gentium* 1.7, 128.
6. *Lumen Gentium* 1.8, 130.

According to Dulles, institutionalism is a corrupt form of ecclesiology, "a deformation of the true nature of the Church."[7] This does not mean that an adequate ecclesiology does not need to account for the institutional aspects of the church. But *institutionalism*, which "defines the Church primarily in terms of its visible structures" does not take adequately into account the inner nature of the church's mystery because of its focus on "external, institutional features."[8] This form of ecclesiology is too juridical, hierarchical, and clerical; it does not give sufficient room for the other aspects of the church, which any adequate ecclesiology must address, according to Dulles.

Dulles suggests that an ecclesiology of the church as mystical communion responds to an exaggerated institutionalism. "Since the institutional categories, as we have seen, cannot do justice to the full reality of the church, it is to be expected that theologians would turn to" a discussion of the church as *Gemeinschaft* (community) when ecclesiology had been dominated by discussion of the church as *Gesellschaft* (society).[9] He highlights the work of Dominican Jerome Hamer who critiques Bellarmine's "definition that would characterize the Church only in terms of its external, institutional features."[10] Hamer prefers the idea of mystical communion to combine the institutional and mystical aspects of the church. Dulles quotes Hamer, that "the mystical body of Christ, is a communion which is at once inward and external, an inner communion of spiritual life (of faith, hope, and charity) signified and engendered by an external communion in profession of the faith, discipline and the sacramental life."[11] It is important to see that Dulles still narrates the controversy in terms of the inner (spiritual, invisible) aspects of the church versus the external (institutional, visible) aspects. For Hamer, and others, as Dulles says, "The outward and visible bonds of a brotherly society are an element in the reality of the Church, but they rest upon a deeper spiritual communion of grace or charity."[12] Even though this is what the theologians of the mystical communion tried to accomplish, Dulles judges their project

7. Dulles, *Models*, 27.

8. Ibid., 41.

9. Ibid., 39.

10. Ibid., 41.

11. Ibid., 41–42.

12. Ibid., 42.

problematic insofar as it does not adequately relate these two dimensions. "Notwithstanding the many advantages, these communal types of ecclesiology suffer from certain weaknesses." He continues,

> For one thing, they leave some obscurity regarding the relationships between the spiritual and visible dimensions of the Church. If the Church is seen totally as a free spontaneous gift of the Spirit, the organizational and hierarchical aspect of the Church runs the risk of appearing superfluous. . . . Official Roman Catholic teaching, in our view, does well to stress the divine value of both the organizational and the communal aspects of the Church and their mutual complementarity. But the communion ecclesiology does not by itself provide any basis for a convincing answer to the arguments of a Brunner or Tillich, who would separate the visible from the spiritual, and look upon the latter alone as the properly divine or religious element.[13]

It is clear that for Dulles one of the chief challenges facing an adequate ecclesiology is to hold together in "mutual complementarity" the two aspects of the church, the invisible and visible, the spiritual and the institutional. Ecclesiologies of mystical communion, while in his view far superior to institutionalism, fail in the opposite direction.

Not surprisingly, Dulles thinks the notion of the church as sacrament helps to overcome the tension presented in the previous two models. "In order to bring together the external and internal aspects into some intelligible synthesis . . . many twentieth century Catholic theologians have appealed to the concept of the Church as sacrament."[14] Dulles writes:

> As a sacrament the Church has both an outer and an inner aspect. The institutional or structural aspect of the Church—its external nature—is essential, since without it the Church would not be visible. . . . On the other hand, the institutional or structural aspect is never sufficient to constitute the Church. The offices and rituals of the Church must palpably appear as the actual expressions of faith, hope, and love of living men. . . . [S]acrament, as we have been saying, is a sign of grace realizing itself. Sacrament has an event character; it is dynamic. The Church becomes Church insofar as the grace of Christ, operative within it, achieves historical tangibility through the actions of the Church as such.[15]

13. Ibid., 52.
14. Ibid., 56.
15. Ibid., 51.

For Dulles, in the church-as-sacrament model the external, visible aspects of the church are the expression of the grace of Christ active invisibly in the church. This is so because "Christ, as the sacrament of God, contains the grace that he signifies. Conversely, he signifies and confers the grace he contains. In him the invisible grace of God takes on visible form."[16] The church's sacramentality is analogous to Christ's own. The invisible grace of Christ contained in the church finds its expression through the sacramental and other visible aspects of the church's hierarchy, institutional structures, rituals and worship. Thus Dulles concludes,

> In summary, the Church is not just a sign, but a sacrament. Considered as a bare institution, the Church might be characterized as just an empty sign. It could be going through formalities and he a hollow shell rather than a living community of grace. But where the Church as sacrament is present, the grace of Christ will not be absent. The grace, seeking its appropriate form of expression—as grace inevitably does—will impel men to prayer, confession, worship, and other acts whereby the Church externally realizes its essence. Through these actions the Church signifies what it contains and contains what it signifies. In coming to expression the grace of the Church realizes itself as grace.[17]

I want to highlight three things about Dulles's view of the Church as sacrament. First, he thinks this view overcomes the tensions created in the juxtaposition of the two previous views. Second, he shows that the dichotomies involved in the tension between the previous two views are not somehow overcome or reinterpreted by the sacramental view; rather, the sacramental view finds a way to relate the visible and invisible, the external and the internal in a new way that takes both seriously but *without questioning these dichotomies themselves*. Finally, the way these two aspects of the church are related is through a theology of grace. Grace becomes the name of the internal/invisible, that which is *contained* by the visible/institutional and which finds expression in the church's external reality. This understanding of grace is paralleled in his theology of the incarnation. Somehow in the incarnation the visible Christ "signifies and confers the grace he contains."[18] These aspects of Dulles's discussion are important to highlight because, while McCabe's early writing on the

16. Ibid., 60.

17. Ibid., 62–63.

18. Ibid., 60.

church and the sacraments is in continuity with the church-as-sacrament approach, he also finds ways to call into question this very way of describing the church as a sacrament.

McCabe's Early Ecclesiological Writings

McCabe's *The New Creation* was published in 1964—the year *Lumen Gentium* was promulgated—but it was published in the United States as *The People of God*. This title is important because it is one of the most popular expressions post-Vatican II for the church, and indeed it is the title of chapter 2 of *Lumen Gentium*. In that chapter the church is related to each of the seven sacraments. Similarly, in *The People of God* McCabe argues that the church is constituted by sacraments. Thus even the title suggests that the discussions of ecclesiology surrounding and coming out of Vatican II create the appropriate context for understanding McCabe's own approach to the church and the sacraments.

Furthermore, the book itself is about how the sacraments constitute the church as a sacrament of human unity and of humanity's unity with God. As we will see below, McCabe considers the divisions of humanity, the failure of humanity to achieve unity, to be the chief sign of human sin. He begins *The People of God*, "We are born with a constitutional inability to live together in love; we achieve a precarious unity only with great difficulty and for a short time; there is a flaw in the very flesh we have inherited which makes for division among us."[19] For McCabe, as for *Lumen Gentium*, the sacraments—and the church in general—are sacraments of human unity; they make present sacramentally the future unity of all humanity, a unity achieved not by humanity's own struggle, but by God's gift of Jesus Christ. As McCabe writes,

> This book is a study of the sacraments as mysteries of human unity, as the way in which men are able to break down the barriers between them and form a real community. It is a study, therefore, of the sacraments as constituting the Church for the Church is nothing but the community which sacramentally foreshadows the life for which God has destined man. She is, so to speak, a living picture of the unity that God has in store for the human race. But she is not just a picture; because Christ is risen her mysteries do

19. McCabe, *People*, ix.

not simply show forth something in the future, they also partially realize something that is present.[20]

Clearly, if Dulles were taking into account McCabe's work, he would discuss it in the chapter on the church-as-sacrament, for McCabe's work is an exploration of the sacraments from the perspective of those activities that make the church the church. Furthermore, McCabe employs the dichotomy of visible/invisible community to suggest that he understands the very problem posed by Dulles—that of relating the institutional/external aspect of the church with the spiritual/internal aspect—when he writes, "Thus, the Church is not simply the visible organization of men and institutions in the sense that a political community is a visible organization; nor, on the other hand, is her reality found in some quite invisible community—the community of those who actually love God, or the community of the predestined. In the same way, the sacraments are not simply external gestures that can be seen by anyone, nor is their reality something purely invisible."[21] If we think back to Gustafson's account of the church, in which he outlined the church's social practices to highlight how they are like the practices of other institutions, it looks like McCabe is using the notion of the sacramentality of the church to provide a richer account.

Even as early as 1964, and even when to all initial appearances McCabe is adopting the approach set forth in *Lumen Gentium* and as described by Avery Dulles, there are important indications that he is unsatisfied with the terms of that approach, especially the inner-invisible/external-visible distinction and Dulles's description of sacraments as containers of and expressions of grace. At least, because of his schooling in Aquinas, Marx, and Wittgenstein, McCabe thinks the issues are much more complicated. Two aspects to this early discussion of the sacraments lay the groundwork for his account of the Eucharist as language and show intimations of his difference with the church-as-sacrament approach as described by Dulles.

First, the quotation above, in which McCabe says that the church is neither simply a "visible organization" nor an "invisible community" and that the sacraments are neither merely "external gestures" nor are they "purely invisible" does *not* end by trying to posit the appropriate relation-

20. McCabe, *People*, xii.
21. Ibid., xiii.

ship between those two aspects—visible and invisible—to get the right balance. As he continues, "Both of the Church and of the sacraments we have to say that they exist at some intermediate level, or at least that they cannot exhaustively be described at either level. In a sense the purpose of this book is to draw attention to this intermediate level of reality, for here the Church and the sacraments are one; the sacraments show themselves as different aspects of the life of the Church; the Church appears as the great sacrament, the mystery of Christ's presence amongst us."[22] For McCabe the intermediate reality of the church and the sacraments is a special characteristic of the church *in via*, for they are the partial realization of the last things in the era that "is neither, like that of the Old Testament, simply prior to the new creation, nor yet fully present to it. The sacraments are the ways in which the last things are partially realized, the intersection of the new world and the world made out of date by the resurrection of Christ."[23] I am not suggesting that McCabe drops the language of visibility and invisibility, of exteriority and interiority—though he does in his discussion of the Eucharist as language. Nonetheless, in his pointing to the eschatological aspect of the sacrament—an aspect that might be invisible to the unbeliever who sees only "the outer fringes of things," but is visible to the believer who "sees the sacraments for what they are" with the eyes of faith[24]—McCabe complicates the notions of interiority and exteriority so important to Dulles's telling of the story of ecclesiology by placing them in an eschatological horizon.

Second, there is no hint in McCabe that sacraments are about containing or expressing grace in the external activities of the church, as in Dulles. For McCabe the Eucharist as a sacrament puts us in contact with the body of Christ. McCabe expressly rejects the interiorizing of the sacrament when he writes:

> There can be no doubt that in recent centuries the physical bodily aspect of our beliefs have been heavily played down. Partly because of philosophical mistakes, we have got into the habit of thinking of the real person as an invisible, immaterial being. Bodily actions are thought to be at best merely manifestations of the real human acts which take place invisibly. Thus we have tried to make morality merely a matter of motives and intentions and other "acts of

22. Ibid., xiii–xiv.
23. Ibid., xiv.
24. Ibid., 69.

the mind"; physical acts have been thought of as morally good or bad only in virtue of their relationship to these interior acts. In a parallel way some people have tried to make of heaven a "state of mind"; the emphasis has been all on the immortality of the soul, while the primary Christian teaching on the resurrection of the body has been pushed well into the background.[25]

McCabe's point in highlighting this "philosophical mistake" is to suggest that the purpose of the sacraments, and especially the sacrament of the Eucharist, is not to dispense grace to the invisible soul of the believer, but to put our bodies in contact with Christ's resurrected body in a real, sacramental way. He writes, "Through the sacramental life of the Church we reach to a living union with the humanity of Christ, but this of its nature carries us on to his divinity, and even the divinity of the Son is not the terminus, for his whole being is to be a relation to the Father."[26] That is what for McCabe makes the church present and one while also comprising McCabe's way of understanding our participation in the divine life as bodies united to the body of the Son. As he says, "It is our presence to the risen Christ that makes us one community; the Eucharist and the sacraments that surround it constitute the Church," and in this presence "there is a genuine human presence involving our bodies and his."[27] In *The People of God*, McCabe begins to show the distinctiveness of his own approach in relationship to the broader trend in ecclesiology in which he is situated. His emphasis on the church as those bodies present sacramentally to the body of Christ subverts the dominant discussion of the inner/outer aspects of the church in a way parallel to his critique of interiority in human anthropology.

The most important argument of this chapter is to show how McCabe's particular account of participation provides an alternative to accounts of the church that posit a visible/invisible or interior/exterior duality. For McCabe, participation in God is participation in God's self-communication through the body of Jesus. Already in his early work in ecclesiology this approach begins to emerge.

25. Ibid., 65.
26. Ibid., xiv.
27. Ibid., 66.

ELEMENTS OF MCCABE'S THEOLOGY: ANTHROPOLOGY AND CHRISTOLOGY

There are two aspects of McCabe's theological vision that need at least brief exploration before we turn to look at his eucharistic theology. They are his Wittgensteinian-Thomistic understanding of humans as embodied minds and his Chalcedonian Christology.[28] Though it is in the discussion of McCabe's eucharistic theology that we will see the specific details of his vision of participation as the bodily practicing of our life in God through Christ and the Spirit—or, in his language, our communication with God and one another in the language of the future—these two aspects of his theology need to be explored because they outline the nature of the very humanity that participates in God, the unknowable God in whom we participate, and the fundamental christological position that "the only God who matters is the unfathomable mystery of love because of which there is being and meaning to anything that is; and that we are united with God in matter, in our flesh and his flesh."[29]

McCabe's Wittgensteinian-Thomism

McCabe's Wittgensteinian-Thomistic anthropology is crucial for understanding the theory of language that undergirds his eucharistic theology and also his understanding of the humans who are joined to God in the flesh of Christ through the Eucharist. His way of viewing humanity and the meaning of human communication lies at the heart of his distinctive contribution to eucharistic theology and thus lies at the center of the argument of this chapter. His account of human beings as embodied minds constitutes the central thrust of his preferred way of thinking about humanity. Since McCabe's Wittgensteinian-Thomistic anthropology is worked out most fully in conversations around the meaning of ethics, the following discussion will display his anthropology in terms of his ethics.

Taking his cue from the shift in analytic philosophy made possible by Wittgenstein's *Philosophical Investigations*, McCabe approaches ethics from the perspective of a changed understanding of language and meaning. He critiques a dualistic theory of meaning according to which, as he says, "The interior mind is the home of concepts and it is where

28. Some parts of the following account of McCabe have been previously published in Owens, "Theological Ethics of Herbert McCabe."

29. McCabe, *God Matters*, preface.

thinking takes place; actions, however, words, and other expressions of my thinking take place in the public world of the body. My words consist of public signs that stand for private thoughts."[30] It is precisely McCabe's Wittgensteinian-Thomism that furnishes him with the critique of this position and an alternative to it. From Wittgenstein McCabe learned that "such problems dissolve once we recognize that what we call concepts are nothing like experiences but are simply skills in the use of words. . . . The question of meaning is not a question about my secret thoughts but about the public language."[31] The meaning of words cannot simply be determined by the thoughts within my head, but meaning is at least quasi-objective, residing not in the mind but in the public use of language and a shared form of life. He writes:

> Meanings, then, are ways of entering into social life, ways of being with each other. The kind of meanings available in the language of a society—taking "language" in its widest extent to include all conventionally determined signs and symbols—constitute the way in which people are with each other in that community. "To imagine a language," as Wittgenstein says, "is to imagine a form of life."[32]

McCabe's Wittgensteinian critique of this dualistic account of language allows him to offer an alternative account of human embodiment. Rather than being an instrument used to express internally produced meanings (or intentions), our bodies are "intrinsically communicative."[33] He writes, "It is not just that the human body can produce speech and writing: all its behaviour is in some degree linguistic. The range of bodily activity that we call man's 'behaviour' consists of those actions which are significant in this way. . . . A piece of human behaviour is not simply an action that gets something *done*, it also has meaning, it gets something *said*."[34] As with the meanings of words, the meanings of our actions, for

---

30. McCabe, *Law*, 84–85.

31. Ibid., 86–87.

32. Ibid., 84.

33. Ibid., 91.

34. Ibid., 91–92. John Howard Yoder takes a very similar position with regard to the intrinsic communicative nature of deeds. For instance, he writes, "Much of the achievement of the civil rights movement in the United States must be understood by means of this category of symbolic evaluation [in which the meaning of the deed is what it signifies]. A sit-in or march is not instrumental but it is *significant*. Even when no immediate change in the social order can be measured, even when persons and organizations have

McCabe, cannot be determined solely by what goes on inside the agent (the intention) but rather with the public, embodied nature of the action as it is performed in a linguistically constituted community.

McCabe realizes that most ways of doing ethics are preeminently concerned with judging the rightness or wrongness, the goodness or badness, of human behavior. Whether this is determined by considering the behavior's consequences or by whether a certain behavior has broken an inviolable law, the most prevalent forms of ethics are all playing in the same ballpark. In this game, ethics seeks to address quandaries; it judges behavior as right or wrong. McCabe's discussion of ethics as language, however, and his extension of language to include the intrinsically communicative nature of all shared bodily life, allows him to offer an alternative account of ethics. Ethics, for McCabe, is precisely the study of human behavior as communicative:

> Now ethics is just the study of human behaviour in so far as it is a piece of communication, in so far as it says something or fails to say something. This does not mean that ethics is uninterested in behaviour in so far as it gets something done, that ethics is not concerned with the consequences of my acts, but its precise concern is with my action as meaningful.[35]

Ethics is the literary criticism of bodily communication. Trying to decide whether a piece of behavior is good or bad, right or wrong, is analogous to saying that the job of literary criticism is to pronounce a poem good or bad. If literary criticism allows one to move more deeply into the significance of a piece of literature, and thus to enjoy it in a non-superficial way, so "the purpose of ethics is similarly to enable us to enjoy life more by responding to it more sensitively, by entering into the significance of human action."[36] Some actions we will find to be shallow and unworthy of our time (McCabe happens to think that this is the kind of behavior capitalist economies condemn us to), and some behavior will reveal deeper and deeper levels of significance. "So I want to say," he writes, "that there is no such thing as *the* moral level. Moral judgements do not consist in

not yet been moved to take a different position, the efficacy of the deed is first of all its efficacy as sign" (Yoder, *Original Revolution*, 161). Again, even more similar to McCabe: "Our deeds must be measured not only by whether they fit certain rules, nor by the results they hope to achieve, but by what they 'say,'" 41.

35. McCabe, *Law*, 92.

36. Ibid., 95.

seeing something at 'the moral level' or 'in light of morality'; it consists in the process of trying to see things always at a yet deeper level."[37] What we find when we do this kind of literary criticism of human life together in light of humanity's divine orientation is that these deeper levels of meaning point to ever more human ways of living. Sometimes we will find that in "some activities a man has not lived into his medium, his action has made sense at some superficial level of meaning but it does not make full human sense."[38] The job of ethics is to help us discover this "full human sense"; to live morally is the attempt to live at the most human level of meaning.[39]

For McCabe, then, ethics is the study of the bodily presence of humans to one another, of human communication, in the community of humanity. McCabe, in fact, is writing primarily of the church, which for him is the sacrament of the eschatological unity of all humanity. When we realize with McCabe that human unity is not a given of our nature but "that human unity is something towards which we move, a goal of history,"[40] then we realize that his ethics is distinctively Christian because the humanity about whose bodily communication McCabe writes is an eschatological reality. As McCabe says, "The fact that mankind is split into fragments which are in imperfect communication with each other means that within these fragments, too, full communication is not achieved."[41] Human unity will be achieved in the eschatological future when our communication, our shared bodily life, is most fully human, lived in perfect fellowship with one another and with God in a way that is not predicated on exclusion, as our fragmented communities are now.

Until then, the world has the church as the sign of its eschatological future. McCabe writes, "Jesus Christ is himself the medium in which men will in the future communicate, he is the body in which we shall all be interrelated members . . . he is the language in which we shall express ourselves to each other in accordance with the promise and summons of the Father. Now this language, this medium, this expression, this body

37. Ibid., 97.
38. Ibid., 100.
39. Ibid., 102.
40. Ibid., 67.
41. Ibid., 99.

which belongs to the future is made really present for us in the church."[42] Through the sacraments of the church Jesus is present bodily as the language of the future. "I mean that the church makes the presence of Christ articulate as a language, as an interpretation of the world, as a means of communication"[43]

For McCabe, intention and action are embodied human communication, meaningful in their public expression in the community of humanity. Since this humanity is fragmented, however, intention and action find their fullest, deepest, most human significance in the sacramental life of the church as it articulates to the world the truth of the world's future unity. "The resurrection meant not just that a church was founded, it meant that the world was different: the church exists to articulate this difference, to show the world to itself."[44] McCabe argues that human communication cannot be achieved until all humanity shares bodily the life of God. Until then, we share now sacramentally in that life through the eucharistic celebration. At the end of *Law, Love and Language*, McCabe writes:

> I have not, in this book, tried to apply christian principles to particular moral questions because it seems to me that christiantiy does not in the first place propose a set of moral principles. As I suggested in my first chapter [on situation ethics], I do not think that such principles are out of place in christianity; without them the notion of love may collapse into vagueness or unmeaning, but christianity is essentially about our communication with each other in Christ, our participation in the world of the future.[45]

McCabe's Christology

It should be clear from my earlier discussions of Cyril of Alexandria and Bonhoeffer that issues of Christology are crucial to understanding accounts of participation. The case is no different for McCabe. Furthermore, as we shall see, McCabe's description of Jesus as God's communication with the world through the language of the future can only make sense as an elucidation of Chalcedonian Christology.

42. Ibid., 141.
43. Ibid., 142.
44. Ibid.
45. Ibid., 172.

Following Aquinas, McCabe advocates an apophatic approach to God—that God's nature is unknowable precisely because God and creatures do not inhabit the same universe (God inhabits no universe). On the surface it could appear that an apophatic theology would make it impossible to speak of God's involvement in the world, of God's relationship to creatures, and of God's taking creatures into God's own life, which we have seen clearly McCabe thinks happens in the sacraments of the church. For McCabe, the doctrine of the incarnation as formulated at Chalcedon and as interpreted by Aquinas is precisely meant to point us to the mystery of the man Jesus who was God's involvement in the world and the hope of our involvement in God without contradicting the unknowability of God. Indeed, the incarnation, for McCabe, does not change this apophatic understanding of God:

> I should add at this point, perhaps, that the revelation of God in Jesus in no way, for Aquinas, changes this situation. By the revelation of grace, he says, we are joined to God as to an unknown, *ei quasi ignoto coniungamur* (ST Ia, 12, 13, ad 1). God remains the mystery which could only be known by God himself, or by our being taken up to share in his own knowledge of himself, a sharing which for us in this world is not knowledge but the darkness of faith.[46]

This is precisely the sharing that happens in the incarnation: Jesus, the divine Word, the divine self-understanding, makes it possible for humans to share in divinity, through the Holy Spirit, so that humans are taken into the divine knowledge and joy that is nothing other than the life of God's triunity. McCabe writes,

> To be able, through faith, to share in Christ, in God's understanding of himself, to be in Christ, is to be filled ourselves also with this joy, this Holy Spirit.... We have a life in us, an understanding and a joy in us, that is too great for us to comprehend. Quite often it has to show itself as what seems its opposite, as darkness and suffering. The Word of God is Christ crucified. But it is God's way and the truth of God and the life and joy of God. And this is in us because we have faith. We have been prepared to go into the dark with Christ, to do with Christ. And we know that this means that we live in Christ. And that life, the divine understanding and the joy that is in us, will one day soon show itself in us for what it truly

46. McCabe, *God Matters*, 41–42.

is. And we shall live with the Father, through the understanding which is the Word made flesh, in the joy which is the Holy Spirit for eternity.[47]

Thus this incarnation is the way of our sharing the life of God, our participation in God, both now through the sacraments of the church (which itself is the sacrament of God's presence), as we have already seen, and eschatologically, when the sacramental system will be no more. McCabe's interpretation of Chalcedon is his way of speaking about God's involvement in the world that leads to our involvement in God. His account of the incarnation has three aspects: 1) the position that he is arguing against; 2) his interpretation of Chalcedon, following Aquinas; and 3) his interpretation of what it means for Jesus to be human in all respects and yet without sin.

McCabe's published reflections on the incarnation have been primarily reactive; they have been precipitated by theological events of the twentieth century. The first is less an event than a movement. McCabe was very critical of process theology (and other theological movements) that try to show how God is an active participant in the world without respecting the distinction between creator and creature and all that distinction implies. These theologians try to find a way to speak of God's involvement in the world and God's suffering with the creation. What they miss, according to McCabe, is that Chalcedonian Christology gives us a way to speak quite literally of God's suffering as a human being. But since these theologians often deny the divinity of Jesus in any sense recognizable by classical Christianity, they cannot accept the incarnation as the best picture of God's involvement in the world. McCabe writes that,

> since there is a profound Christian instinct that the gospel has to do with the suffering of God, these theologians are constrained to say that since God did not literally suffer in Jesus, God must suffer in some other way; as, for example, he surveys the suffering of Jesus and the rest of mankind. One consequence of this, of course, is that whereas a traditional Christian would say that God suffered a horrible pain in his hands when he was nailed to the cross, these theologians have to make do with a kind of mental anguish at the follies and sins of creatures.[48]

47. McCabe, *God Still Matters*, 106.
48. McCabe, *God Matters*, 46.

This latter picture of God's suffering is the picture that we have seen McCabe finds incompatible with the Christian notion of an impassible God. The former picture of God's suffering—in his hands on a tree—however, is perfectly within the bounds of orthodox Christian speech if one takes seriously the Council of Chalcedon.

The second event to which McCabe responds is the publication of *The Myth of God Incarnate*. This book is a collection of essays by notable authors who critique the church's doctrine of the incarnation as undermining the humanity of Jesus. In a withering critique of the book McCabe spells out his own interpretation of the incarnation and clarifies the meaning and point of the Chalcedonian definition.

What, according to McCabe (who claims he is following Aquinas), is it about the dogma of the hypostatic union of the divine and human natures in the one person Jesus that makes us able to say quite literally, "God suffered a horrible pain in his hands" but prevents us from saying that God experienced the "overhearing of transistor radios or drinking Coke"?[49] He summarizes the answer succinctly when he writes:

> Part of the doctrine of the incarnation is precisely that Jesus was and is a human person; the other part is that this same identical person was and is divine. The adjectives "divine" and "human" express *what* Jesus is (his nature), the name "Jesus" refers to *who* (which person) he is. In virtue of his human nature certain things can be asserted or denied about Jesus; in virtue of his divine nature certain other things can be asserted or denied of him, but all these assertions are about one person. The point is a logical one (or as these authors [of *The Myth of God Incarnate*] prefer to call it, a "metaphysical" one). Thus it is true to say "God died on the cross" or "God suffered hunger and thirst" because in these sentences "God" is . . . indicating the subject, the person, about whom the assertion is being made.[50]

This summary is the heart of McCabe's point, but it requires elaboration.

For McCabe, the questions of Christology are mainly questions about language. What statements are appropriately said about Christ given the unity of the divine and the human in the person of Jesus Christ? What utterances are allowed and disallowed? For McCabe, dogmas like the definition of Chalcedon are in many ways primarily rules for speech, their

49. Ibid., 48.
50. Ibid., 56.

job being to rule out inappropriate statements, statements that contradict the mystery, though they themselves neither explain nor define the mystery. Aquinas's treatment of Chalcedon, according to McCabe, relies on a particular way of understanding how sentences work. "Without going too far into this," McCabe writes, "what [Aquinas] means is that the subject words are there to stand for, to identify what you are talking about, to refer, while the words of the predicate are there to say something about it, they are taken as to their meaning."[51] The word in the subject position is a pointer, used to identify, not to describe. McCabe offers an example: "Now consider the proposition 'God sat down by the well.' This for Aquinas is a perfectly proper and true utterance since 'God' is one of the ways in which you could identify Jesus; 'God', here, is in the subject place and is being used to identify what is being talked about."[52]

There is for Aquinas an important qualification; the word *qua* can change the whole meaning and render an otherwise true utterance false. The word *qua* ("in virtue of being") makes whatever follows part of the predicate, part of what is being said about the subject. McCabe continues with his example: "But if you said 'Jesus *qua* God sat down by the well' it would be very different. This would assert (1) that Jesus sat by the well, and (2) that Jesus is God, and (3) that it is because of being God that he sat by the well. Now since the third of these is false the original proposition is false." He continues:

> The word "*qua*" is important because we are to be concerned with natures, and a nature is that in virtue of which things are true of a thing, or can be said of a thing. To say that Jesus has two natures is to say that he has, so to say, two *quas*. He does some things *qua* human and others *qua* divine. This does not mean that he has two sources of power and could switch form one to the other, like having an emergency engine on a sailing boat. It means that there are two levels of talking about him, or that he exists at two levels.[53]

Whatever can be said of Jesus as a subject can rightly be said of God. "God suffered." "God was thirsty." "God is a man." All of these are true because "God" here points to Jesus who is both God and human. "A man is God." "A man forgives sins." "A man heals." These statements also are true

51. McCabe, *God Still Matters*, 108.
52. Ibid., 109.
53. Ibid., 109–10.

precisely because, again, "man" here points to Jesus, who did these things as the one *hypostasis* in whom are joined divine and human natures. This understanding of the incarnation comprises McCabe's answer to those who want to advocate for God's involvement in the world in terms of a general theory of God's suffering or compassion. The incarnation allows McCabe to maintain that God does not have experiences *qua* God—God does not learn, have compassion, etc., as we have seen—but God *qua* Jesus suffered and experienced all that Jesus suffered and experienced precisely because the one person Jesus is both God and a human.

Why is this discussion of Christology important for McCabe's eucharistic theology and an account of bodily participation in God? In the preface to *God Matters*, McCabe writes, "In the end, I suppose, I am only trying to say two not very original things: that the only God who matters is the unfathomable mystery of love because of which there is being and meaning to anything that is; and that we are united with God in matter, in our flesh and his flesh." For McCabe, our participation in the divine—our union with God—is a matter of the flesh, of our bodies, indeed of bodily participation. His understanding of participation is not conceived abstractly apart from the incarnation, an incarnation that allows us to say that God has flesh to which we can be united. That unity, as we shall see, comes through the sacramental constitution of the church, and especially the church's eucharistic practice. As McCabe writes of the Eucharist, "It is his [Jesus'] own body and blood that constitute the People of God; they are to form one people just in so far as their bodies are linked with his. ... [W]e belong to the new human race because our bodies are linked with the risen body of Christ."[54]

There is one final aspect to McCabe's account of Jesus that we need to consider. The definition of Chalcedon is quite clear: Jesus was human in every respect, that is, like us except without sin. According to McCabe, "To say that Jesus was without sin just means that he was wholly loving, that he did not put up barriers against people, that he was not afraid of being at the disposal of others, that he was warm and free and spontaneous."[55] This means that Jesus was able to relate to others in a way that he could be totally present, without exclusion. In a world where human unity is predicated on exclusion—as McCabe says, "This world is held together mainly

54. McCabe, *People*, 65.
55. McCabe, *God Still Matters*, 96.

by the common ties between its members but there is also the important fact of exclusiveness. It is held together not only by love but also by fear, one of its bonds is a common hostility to what is alien"—Jesus himself presents a new way of relating, a way without barriers, a way "unmixed with domination or exclusiveness."[56] This according to McCabe leads to Jesus's death, for in such a world "the only way to get by is to restrict your humanity rather carefully. . . . Now Jesus did not ration his love, so naturally he didn't last."[57]

As I have said, McCabe interprets the Eucharist in terms of language, of communication; indeed, as we have already seen, he interprets all of bodily life in terms of communication, for our bodies, as he says, "are intrinsically communicative."[58] The situation of humanity, the limited unity that individuals find with each other and that societies experience as predicated on a degree of exclusion and domination, is interpreted as a failure of communication, as a failure of humanity to achieve bodily presence to one another in a way that does not imply exclusion and absence. The same is true for Jesus; before the resurrection, Jesus lived a fully human life, a life without domination or exclusion, but he was limited bodily. His presence in one place implied an absence in another. After the resurrection, through the sacramental constitution of the church, Jesus is, as McCabe says, *more* bodily because now his presence does not also imply an absence.[59] So the church becomes a community based on a new mode of communication, the communication made possible by the body of Jesus in which we share.

THE EUCHARIST AS LANGUAGE

McCabe critiques dualistic philosophical and anthropological notions of interiority based on a Wittgensteinian-Thomistic understanding of humans as embodied minds and bodies as intrinsically communicative. Insofar as this dualistic anthropology has analogies in ecclesiologies that try to define the nature of the church by striking the right balance between

---

56. McCabe, *Law*, 128–29.

57. McCabe, *God Still Matters*, 97.

58. McCabe, *Law*, 91.

59. We have already seen that for Bonhoeffer "body" means availability. In the next chapter we will see that Robert Jenson's account of participation hangs on a similar account of what it means to be "body."

the inner, invisible essence and its outer, visible manifestation, McCabe thinks those very ecclesiologies are insufficient to account for the bodily significance of the church and for how the church in its bodily communion with Christ shares in the life of God. I now turn to a discussion of McCabe's account of the Eucharist, which will round out the argument. Here McCabe uses the language of communication to reinterpret traditional accounts of eucharistic transubstantiation precisely for the purpose of showing how in the practice of Eucharist the church's embodiment is joined to God's own embodiment as we participate in the body of the Son, God's self-communication.

McCabe was at once a creative theologian and also deeply faithful to the theological tradition of the Roman Catholic church. This creativity as a faithful expression of the church's teaching is most clear in his constructive theological reflections on the meaning and role of the eucharistic celebration within the church. Remarking that the Catholic Church has no official teaching on the Eucharist—"The Council of Trent," he reminds us, "did not decree that Catholics should believe in transubstantiation: it just called it a most appropriate way of talking about the Eucharist"[60]—he wants to find a more appropriate way to talk about the Eucharist, one that gets at what the older teaching was getting at, but only better, and one that avoids two extremes. He fears that a certain way of viewing the Eucharist, one of the extremes, is rampant among Catholic Christians. McCabe suggests that most Catholics believe that at the consecration of the elements the bread and the wine change into a different kind of thing, a different substance, on the lines of a chemical change. They are no longer bread and wine; now they are Jesus's body and blood sitting on a table. The mystery, on this view, is that they do not look like flesh and blood. Jesus's flesh and blood are disguised as bread and wine—they maintain the appearances of bread and wine. "This is so that," he suggests, "we can eat the flesh and drink the blood of Christ without being disgusted by the cannibalism involved."[61] The main point on this view is that the body and blood, while really there, are under the disguise of bread and wine; they come to the party incognito.[62]

60. McCabe, *God Still Matters*, 115.

61. Ibid., 115.

62. Ibid., 116–17.

The other extreme is the Protestant error (or as McCabe would say, *one* of the Protestant errors). On this view, when we talk about the bread and the wine being the body and blood of Christ, we are speaking "merely metaphorically. Like a crucifix or a religious painting, the food and drink serve as symbols that remind us of Christ and form a focus for our faith in him."[63] The bread and the wine are no different from any other bread and wine; it's just that in this context they serve a different function. Similarly, a "bottle of champagne is just a bottle of champagne, but when it plays a role in a certain ceremony it becomes a Christmas present."[64] We just deem what is on the altar to be the body and blood of Christ, as we deem a piece of stage furniture to be the real thing during the theatrical production.[65] McCabe acknowledges that though the first view is a mistaken Catholic view, any Catholic position must distinguish itself from the latter.

By characterizing these two extremes—the views that a true Catholic position must avoid—he has implicitly outlined the criteria that his view must meet. A true Catholic position must maintain that the bread and the wine undergo such a radical change—a substantial change—that it makes no sense to think of them as ontologically the same as they were before. It is not as if they stay the same and our attitude towards them changes, as with the Champagne bottle that has become a Christmas present. Neither, however, can the eucharistic change be thought of as some sort of chemical change; it is not a disguised bait and switch. As McCabe puts it,

> The view I shall be putting forth is that in the Eucharist the food and drink we enjoy has been radically or, as we say, "substantially," transformed, that it has become the body of Christ. It is not simply a matter of something remaining ontologically the same but acquiring a new significance, nor however is it a matter of something becoming a new chemical substance in a disguised form.[66]

With the alternatives to avoid in place, and McCabe's criteria for what he thinks makes a faithful Catholic account of the notion of eucharistic transubstantiation spelled out, we can look at McCabe's constructive proposals.

63. Ibid., 117.
64. Ibid., 116.
65. Ibid., 117.
66. Ibid.

McCabe's account of the Eucharist begins with a few distinctions. The essential question for the Eucharist is, How is Christ present to us in the Eucharist? This, he suggests, is a different question from, How is Christ's body present to us in the Eucharist? To answer the first question— how Christ is present—any Catholic answer must be, "Christ is present because the food and drink have become his body."[67] But this still leaves the second question: How is Christ's body present? The answer to that question is: sacramentally. As McCabe puts it, "'This is the body of Christ' says how Christ is present to us. 'This is the sacrament of Christ's body' says how his body is present to us."[68] As we will see, this becomes a crucial distinction.

The second distinction is between appearances and signs. Appearances are "just there"; they are not deceptive. Appearances simply show themselves and thus show a certain thing. Appearances are, in a way, a raw physical reality. Signs, on the other hand, are part of a system of language; they inhabit the world of human culture. Signs tell, appearances do not. "There is, then," McCabe writes, "a lot of difference between the appearance which simply shows you a thing and signs which are part of telling you something about it."[69] This is a crucial point for understanding what takes place in the consecration of the bread and wine. On the mistaken Catholic view, the appearances of bread and wine become, after consecration, deceptive appearances of something else—the body and blood. According to McCabe (who thinks he is giving a truthful, if updated account in different language, of Aquinas's position), before consecration the appearances of bread and wine are there because bread and wine are there; after consecration, however, they "cease to function as appearances at all, they have become signs, sacramental signs through which what is signified is made real." He continues, "Before the consecration the appearances were there because the bread was there; they were just the appearances of the bread. After consecration it is the other way around; the body of Christ is sacramentally there because what were the appearances of bread (and are now sacramental signs), are there."[70] So the distinction between appearances and signs is the way McCabe makes sense of the

67. Ibid.
68. Ibid., 117.
69. Ibid., 118.
70. Ibid.

previous distinction between the presence of Christ and the presence of Christ's body; Christ is present because his body is present; his body is present because what were the appearances of bread and wine have become the sacramental signs of Christ's body. And for McCabe there is one more crucial step to round out this account:

> When we do things to the host, such as eating it, we are not doing anything to Christ's body. What we are doing is completing the significance of the signs. For bread and wine are meant to be eaten and drunk, to be our food; and food, eating and drinking together is, even in our secular lives, a sign expressing friendship and unity. This is why Jesus chose it to be the sign which would tell us of the real sacramental presence of his body given for us and his blood poured our for us—the body of Christ which is more deeply food, our "bread and wine," than is ordinary bread and wine which we began.[71]

The bread and the wine are now sacramental signs for Christ's body and blood; and Christ chose to become food for us as a way of expressing how deeply he is present. He became food for us because around the table we are most deeply present to one another and united. Thus when the bread and the wine change into the body and blood of Christ, they become more deeply food—more deeply our unity and peace and nourishment—than they ever were before.

To try to make sense of this—"the food is more food than it was before"—McCabe proposes an analogy. The Marxist in him—and his Marxism runs almost as deep as his Wittgeininianism and his Thomism—wants to view the eucharistic change in terms of radical, revolutionary change. Consider a society, Britain for instance. This society has certain structures that make it British, certain traditions and histories. Many might see that these structures and traditions are corrupt and need to be changed. Some advocate from within the system for change, tweaking it here and tweaking it there. Others want a revolution, where it is impossible to see what the society will look like in the future after the revolution; but they know that the change necessary must be the death of the structures and the traditions as they currently are. For McCabe, there are a few things to notice about these revolutionaries. First, they often, while in the minority, express the deepest desires of the people for a truer, more

---

71. Ibid., 118. That the signification is only complete when the communicants eat is the beginning of an account of how the Eucharist is a practice.

equal freedom. Fear of the unknown, however, keeps most people want-ing to work within the "system." Second, the revolution, if it takes place, is not just a destruction; it is a death and resurrection. From the standpoint of the new society it must be possible, if it is a true revolution, to look back and re-narrate the history and traditions of that society to show that they are in some kind of continuity with the new, post-revolution society, a continuity it was impossible to foresee before the revolution. What we discover is this: British society post-revolution is more British than it ever was before. The society has become *truly*, deeply British in a way that never could have been imagined within the structures of that society as they were.[72]

How does this analogy apply to the Eucharist? Consider, McCabe suggests, how Jesus was present to Peter. The mode of Jesus's presence—his mode of communication—is his body. Here McCabe makes a broader philosophical point, that our bodies are modes of communication, the way we exist and are present (and absent) to one another.[73] "St. Peter of Galilee might have said, pointing to Jesus in the days of his flesh, 'This is the body of Jesus' and he might have meant, amongst other things, 'This is the way Jesus is present to us.'"[74] Since his resurrection, however, Jesus's body has undergone something like a revolutionary change, so that it is no longer a mode of absence, but only a means of presence; if bodies are how we are present to one another, then Jesus is *more* bodily *after* the resurrection because he can be present bodily without the reverse, without his bodily absence. McCabe suggests that this is precisely the way Christ's body is present to us in the Eucharist, as the communication of Christ among us, since our bodies are our communication. And it can be this communica-tion because Christ's body has undergone death and resurrection so that it is more bodily now—more present, more communicable—that it was before the resurrection, but in a way never imaginable beforehand.[75] "The resurrection means that he has passed through the revolution, he is avail-able in his bodilinesss more than he was, he is now able to be present to all men and not just to a few in Palestine."[76]

---

72. Ibid., 121–23.

73. This point is made much more copiously in McCabe, *Law,* 68–103.

74. McCabe, *God Matters,* 117.

75. Ibid., 117.

76. Ibid., 125.

This, of course, according to McCabe, is the same kind of change the food undergoes on the altar.

> The doctrine of transubstantiation, as I see it, is that the bread and wine suffer a revolutionary change, not that they change into something else, they become more radically food and drink, but this food and drink which is the body of Christ, appears to us still in its traditional dress, so that we will recognize it.[77]

Far from coming to the party incognito, the body and blood of Christ look to us like bread and wine, not to fool us, but precisely so that we will see it for what it really is: the body of Christ sacramentally present in the signs of bread and wine, because the body of Christ is more deeply food for us than bread and wine ever were.

Now that we have introduced the concept of our bodies being communication, we can explore what is the final important way McCabe gives us to understand the Eucharist. To put it briefly, the Eucharist is for McCabe God's language of the future present, among us. The Eucharist is a new language, a new mode of communication because it is the communication of God to us through the body of Christ, and thus becomes a new means of our communication with one another. Eucharist becomes the language of the future by which we communicate with one another through the medium of food, a food that is more food than it ever was before. Our human bodies, as they are, are means of communication, means of being present with one another; but that means they are also the means of exclusion. And it is around the table, eating and drinking, that we most fully enact this unity and this exclusion. The table is most powerful, most significant in human communication, as a communication of welcome, presence, unity; but only so many bodies fit around a table, so its flip side is exclusion. When Christ's body is present to us as a new, resurrected body, sacramentally in the signs of bread and wine, then Christ is present as a new communication, a new language of unity that does not entail exclusion. It is thus the language of the future—how we will communicate and be present to one another and to God after the resurrection when we see God face to face—here with us now, in our midst, constituting the church as the new humanity, waiting for the redemption of its many bodies. McCabe writes,

---

77. Ibid., 126.

THE SHAPE OF PARTICIPATION

In the Eucharist, then, we have an intersection of future and present, we have what is ostensibly language of the present, of this
world, of this body, but which in fact is language of the future, of
the world to come, of the risen body.... In the sacraments then,
we are speaking of the Word of God to express our faith. In this
sense we can say that Christ is present in the Eucharist, say, as the
expression of our faith, as the language in which we communicate
with the Father and with each other.[78]

CONCLUSION

How is McCabe's theology of the Eucharist about participation? McCabe
transforms the traditional language of participation into the language of
communication, so that when we participate, through the incarnation and
the Eucharist, in the Word of the Father, we are participating in God's own
self-communication. But that self-communication is nothing other than
God's own understanding himself through the eternal Word; that is, to
share in God's self-communication is to share in the life of God's triunity.
As McCabe writes, "The word of God is the way in which the Father sees
himself, his realisation of himself; the incarnation means that this divine
self-realisation is shared with us. We are able to enter into the language,
and hence the life, of the Father."[79]

As we have already seen, the failure of human unity is the chief indication of sin; it is our failure to live in loving, self-giving relationship.
Thus, the divine self-sharing in the incarnate Word is also the divine healing of the brokenness and domination that is the plight of humanity. To
share in the life of the Father is to be joined in a new community, and new
humanity. To share in God's self-communication is to be offered a new
mode of human communication precisely because in the incarnation the
communication of God appeared in a body, the organ of human communication. But the communication of the body of Jesus was pure, peaceful
communication in that it was not predicated on violence, exclusion, or
domination. McCabe writes:

> The claim that Jesus is perfectly human is the claim that his social
> world is co-extensive with humanity, that he is open to all men and
> moreover to all that is in man.... [T]he communication he offers

78. Ibid., 128.
79. McCabe, *Law*, 126.

in unmixed with domination or exclusiveness. So the coming of
Jesus would not be just the coming of an individual specimen of
excellent or virtuous man, a figure whom we might try to imitate,
but the coming of a new humanity, a new kind of community
amongst men. For this reason we can compare the coming of Jesus
to the coming of a new language; and indeed, John does this: Jesus
is the word, the language of God which comes to be a language
for man.[80]

There is an immediate connection then between participation in the
life of God—in the self-communication of the Father—and participation
with one another in the new humanity that Jesus gives us. "Jesus is the
future destiny of mankind (to which we are summoned by the Father)
trying to be present amongst men in our present age. He offers a new way
in which they can be free to be themselves, the way of total self-giving, and
he offers this in amongst the various makeshift ways in which men have
tried to build community."[81] The point here is to show that for McCabe,
but to use language slightly different from McCabe's, *participation in God*
in neither abstract nor ideal; it is neither interior nor invisible. Participation
in the life of God is God's sharing his communication with humanity, it is
God's sharing God's own practicing his life with humans so that they might
practice a different life together, an embodied life that looks different from
the embodied exclusion on which human community has hitherto been
founded.

McCabe further highlights the relationship between participation and the practical life of the Christian community in two sermons.
Remember that to participate in Christ is to share in the new mode of
communication he offers and also to share in the life of the Father. Here
McCabe gives shape to that mode of communication:

> We are not optimists; we do not present a lovely vision of the world
> which everyone is expected to fall in love with. We simply have,
> wherever we are, some small local task to do, on the side of justice,
> for the poor. This, in the power of the Spirit we will try to do, and
> we know that to do it is to risk hostility and persecution as Jesus
> risked crucifixion. It is to risk defeat. And this is what we man by
> hope. For our hope is the kind that goes through defeat and cru-
> cifixion to resurrection. We know that we shall sometimes *have* to

80. Ibid., 129.
81. Ibid.

> fail rather than betray the very justice that we struggle for; we shall
> have to fail rather than use the weapons of the oppressor against
> him, but we can do this because we have hope, because we know
> that God will bring life out of such defeat and failure as he brought
> life out of the tomb of Jesus.[82]

Jesus, for McCabe, died of being human. Living a fully human life in a world that must minimize its humanity leads to death. That is what it means for Jesus to be human and that is what it means for Jesus's body to present to the world a new mode of truly human communication. Here we see quite clearly the shape, then, of the church's participation in God, in God's communication of himself. That shape is not unlike the shape of participation we saw in Bonhoeffer's discussion of proclamation: *it is the faithful living a life that looks like the life of Jesus.* As McCabe says, "We are saved by [Jesus's] human sanctity, the grace by which he was wholly obedient to his Father in heaven. We are born into the world of sin, a world of greed, cruelty and selfishness. But by our faith, by our baptism, which is the sacrament of faith, we renounce our citizenship in this world and are dedicated to the world of the future, the world of peace and justice and love."[83]

If the "world of the future" is a world of "peace and justice and love" that are the practical shape of the church, then we can see more clearly what McCabe means when he writes that the "sacramental life is the creative interpretation of the world in terms of the presence to it of Christ, its future."[84] As he says, "The resurrection meant not just that a church was founded, it meant that the world was different: the church exists to articulate this difference, to show the world to itself. We say that the church in the proclamation of the gospel, and in particular in the sacraments, makes Christ, our future, really present but not as though he were previously absent; the difference lies in the mode in which he is present [i.e., sacramentally]."[85] The church is the community articulating—practicing, so to speak—the world's future, thus showing in this practical articulation the shape of the world to come, the shape of the world as it was meant to be, sharing the life of God. The articulation happens primarily in the

---

82. McCabe, *God, Christ and Us*, 15.
83. Ibid., 67.
84. McCabe, *Law*, 143.
85. Ibid., 142–43.

church's sacramental life, and especially in the Eucharist, which makes present to the church Christ's body and thus makes the church the presence of Christ's body to the world, the picture of the world's future, as it practices the fully human life of Christ in peace, justice, and love.

PART THREE

5

Varieties of Participation

IN THIS BOOK I'VE been highlighting two important aspects of ecclesiology. The first is a move to emphasize the *humanness* of the church,
pointing to the embodied social practices that constitute the church's life
as a human institution with a lived, embodied memory. Given some philosophical sophistication by the work of Alasdair MacIntyre, this strand
has recently been conceptualized by the *practices* movement, which has
pointed to the various social practices as crucial ways to understand the
meaning of the life of the church and the life of discipleship. There has also
been a strand in ecclesiology which has aimed at describing the church
in terms of its relationship to God, descriptions that often play off of the
dichotomies of interiority and exteriority and visibility and invisibility. I
argued in Part One that each of these approaches is inadequate, the former
because discussions of the church in terms of practices cannot articulate
how those practices are also God's practices, the active embodiment of the
church's participation in God's life, in a way distinct from creation *qua* creation's participation in God. Similarly, much of the movement to discern
the essence of the church in the church's interior or invisible relationship
to God, however conceived, has done so in a way that makes secondary,
or non-essential to the church, the human practices that constitute the
church's embodiment in the world. Too often the *participating* church is a
disembodied church. I argued that what is required is an account of participation both in terms of God's triunity—because participation is not in
being in general but in the being of God's active, triune life—and in terms
of ecclesial practices, because participation is not the participation of an
interior, disembodied, invisible essence of the church, but of the church
as that body practicing its visibility in the world through its constitutive
social practices. Such an account, I suggested, would have to show how
the church's participation in God is distinct from the rest of creation's

participation in God in order to adequately characterize the relationship between the church and the world.

In Part Two, I looked at two particular ecclesial practices in the hope of finding the possibility of just such an account of participation. I began to articulate an account of the church, drawn from theological accounts of the church's embodied proclamation and eucharistic celebration, that says that the church is Christ's own practicing himself in the Spirit on behalf of the world. And these embodied ecclesial practices *are* Christ's practicing himself in the Spirit, and thus are the church's embodied participation in God's active life as Father, Son, and Holy Spirit. Furthermore, it became clear that if these practices are the church's embodied participation, then that participation will have a visibility; it will have a peculiar shape that will be the church's peaceable-ness.

In this chapter I will answer the question: What is participation and with what accounts of participation does mine differ? So far I have been using the term "participation," but have not yet given it the attention it deserves. Thus, here I outline several recent theological accounts of participation, beginning with the work of John Milbank and Radical Orthodoxy. Perhaps more than anyone else, Milbank's work has retrieved the notion of participation as crucial to his project of overcoming the secular. But other approaches will be surveyed—those of Robert Jenson and Norman Wirzba—because each of these, in its own way, presents a challenge and alternative to Radical Orthodoxy. Then I will turn, in the next chapter, to the work of Maximus the Confessor, who will help me articulate more fully than has yet been done a trinitarian account of participation that takes seriously the practiced embodiment of the church.

In the end I will argue, as I have been arguing, that the church's participation in God is embodied and visible. It is visible in church-constitutive practices as both the signs and the presence of Christ's peaceable existence in the world. Indeed, this embodied, visible participation in God *is* Christ's peaceable existence in the world, as Christ continues to offer himself to the world as the world's true end by practicing himself, in the Spirit, as the church.

VARIETIES OF PARTICIPATION

Participation in John Milbank's Radical Orthodoxy

No discussion of participation can ignore the work of John Milbank and the theological movement Radical Orthodoxy inaugurated by his *Theology and Social Theory*. While Milbank has done more than anyone to bring the theological topic of participation back onto the theological scene, I want to suggest that his account of participation, despite his repeated emphasis on materiality, does not adequately show how an account of participation must begin with Christ and his church and how the church as Christ's body embodies its participation in the world. How we understand the rest of creation's participation in God will take its bearing from the particularity of the church's own participation in God's life as Christ's body drawing the world into God's life through its practices of participation.

In *Theology and Social Theory* Milbank offers a narrative of the rise of the so-called secular social sciences as heretical accounts of creation, accounts that attempted in their various ways to secure for the social sciences an autonomous sphere, untouched by religion. He argues that such social theories need radical theological critique, a critique that involves a recovery of the ancient and medieval Christian and Platonic notion of participation, which says that all that is, precisely because it is, participates in God as God's creation. For Milbank, this notion of creation extends from the being of the world, to human knowing, to the expansive range of human making—human *poiesis*. While the secular social sciences, according to Milbank, have attempted to secure the material world by denying its participation in God, Milbank argues that the integrity of creation can only be maintained by denying the secular through a comprehensive account of all creation's (including human knowing and making) participation in God.[1] There are two aspects of Milbank's account of participation I wish to highlight: 1) participation and being; and 2) participation and making.

PARTICIPATION AND BEING

In the introduction to the edited collection *Radical Orthodoxy*, Milbank, Graham Ward, and Catherine Pickstock write:

---

1. Milbank, *Theology and Social Theory*, 1–100.

> The central theological framework of radical orthodoxy is "participation" as developed by Plato and reworked by Christianity, because any alternative configuration perforce reserves a territory independent of God. The latter can lead only to nihilism (though in different guises). Participation, however, refuses any reserve of created territory, while allowing finite things their own integrity. ... [E]very discipline must be framed from a theological perspective; otherwise these disciplines will define a zone apart from God, grounded literally in nothing.[2]

Their retrieval of a Platonic/Christian understanding of participation, even if they promise to offer an account "more incarnate, more participatory, ... 'more Platonic'" than Plato and the ancient Christian writers, allows them to approach the favorite subjects of the postmodern philosophers—"embodied life, self-expression, sexuality, aesthetic experience, human political community"[3]—from a densely theological perspective in which creation and the whole range of human embodied and sensory life is understood as having its proper integrity, its own depths, precisely because they are *not* secular or reductionistically material; because of their participation in the transcendent they are *more* that what they seem. They write:

> Hence, by appealing to an eternal source for bodies, their art, language, sexual and political union, one is not ethereally taking leave of their density. On the contrary, one is insisting that behind this density resides an even greater density—beyond all contrasts of density and lightness (as beyond all contrasts of definition and limitlessness). This is to say that there is *only* because it is more than it is.[4]

While this participatory metaphysics derives initially from Plato, as it is reworked by Christianity, it has two important differences. For Christianity, in opposition to a Platonic conception of participation, created being is not a declension from an original, monadic being, on a kind of sliding scale of being. The second difference is that, as James Smith says, "Within a Christian theological framework—as distinguished from a merely Platonic notion of *methexis*—this relationship of dependence of creation

---

2. Milbank, et. al., *Radical Orthodoxy*, 3.

3. Ibid., 3.

4. Ibid., 4.

on the Creator could be described in terms of a grace or giftedness."[5] This notion of gift provides a response to those who consider Milbank's participation too platonic:

> It is just *because* things as created can only be as gifts, just because their being is freely derived, that one has to speak of Creation in terms of participation and of analogical likeness of the gift to the giver—since if his mark is not upon the gift, how else shall we know that it is a gift? Those who imagine that participation is for Christian theology some sort of alien Hellenistic theme (besides the fact that they can never have read the Bible with any attention) fail to see just this, as they equally fail to see that for Greek philosophy there is no uncreated material residue that was not created, and so not a gift, and which therefore *limited* the sway of *methexis*.[6]

Milbank's participation is distinguished from Platonic participation because for Milbank participated being is not a declension from an original unitary being, but rather is the graced giftedness of all creation as its being is given from the triune being of God.

PARTICIPATION AND MAKING

If Milbank's account of participation takes its root from an analogical conception of being, he also, as we have seen, wants his account of participation to extend beyond its classical application to being and human knowing to the whole range of human making. Exactly how he accounts for this extension and how he grounds it christologically (in the *poiesis* of the second Person of Trinity) we will see below. Here I want to highlight this further dimension of his account of participation. At the beginning of *The Word Made Strange* Milbank wonders whether it is possible to identify true Christian practice, and in a way laments that the task of describing and identifying true Christian practice "falls on [the theologian's] own head."[7] With such a daring overestimation of the theologian's importance and task, it is no surprise that Milbank's work centers on not only Christian practice, but human practice more generally—the full scope of human making and doing that has, according to Rowan Williams, an irreducible hopefulness about it, which Milbank would call the mark of its

5. Smith, *Introducing Radical Orthodoxy*, 192.

6. Milbank, *Being Reconciled*, xi.

7. Milbank, *Word Made Strange*, 1.

participation.[8] In Augustine, for instance, participation focuses primarily on creation's being as participating in the being of God and as human knowing participating in the knowledge of God.[9] Milbank wants to augment this christologically by suggesting that human making, along with being and knowing, participates in God insofar as it participates in the poetic of the divine Son. As he writes in the preface to *Being Reconciled*:

> Traditionally, *methexis* concerned a sharing of being and knowledge in the Divine. Those who still espouse this perspective tend to play down the importance of language, culture, time and historicity as encouraging relativism incompatible with any vision of a metaphysical order. Those on the other hand who stress these factors tend to do so at the expense of such a vision. Against this dismal alternative, I have always tried to suggest that participation can be extended also to language, history, and culture: the whole realm of human *making*. Not only do being and knowledge participate in a God who is and who comprehends; also human making participates in a God who is infinite poetic utterance: the second person of the Trinity. Thus when we contingently but authentically make things and reshape ourselves through time, we are not estranged from the eternal, but enter further into its recesses by what for us is the only possible route.[10]

Exactly how Milbank associates human making, human *poiesis*, with the poetic of the Son we will discuss below as we look more carefully at a christological essay. At this point I want to note that he makes this move, that it is constitutive of his account of participation, that it is warranted christologically (in a way that participation as being and knowing aren't necessarily), and that it would seem to ground participation's embodiment.[11]

8. Williams, *On Christian Theology*. He writes, "All sign-making is the action of hope, the hope that this world may become other and that its experienced fragmentariness can be worked into sense," (207).

9. Augustines's understanding of being and participation is given with remarkable clarity in Griffiths, *Lying*, 41–54. Griffiths writes, "Your eyes, says Augustine, are participants in God's light. If you close them you don't decrease the light in which your eyes participate; and if you open them you don't increase the light in which they participate. What he says of eyes he says of everything that exists, which is to say that for him the characteristic mark of being is participation: to be is to participate, to be a *particeps*, in God" (41).

10. Milbank, *Being Reconciled*, ix.

11. Paul Griffiths's chapter in *Lying* on "being" in Augustine (see note 9 above) shows

Participation, then, according to Milbank is a theological ontology that grounds the integrity of creation, human knowing, and human making—materiality as both creation and construction—by showing these to be the good gifts of a transcendent God; their giftedness, their being upheld by grace, constitutes the depth and the excess of their being so that they are fundamentally understood as being just insofar as their being derives from and participates in God's own.

In some respects Milbank's conception of participation is crucial for the argument of this book. I too want to deny a univocal conception of being that collapses transcendence into immanence. But is Milbank's the only alternative? I want to pose two questions to Milbank's account of participation and to offer two critical suggestions that point to an ecclesially centered account of participation grounded in the particular participation of Jesus and the church. The first question is: Despite all of its talk about materiality, does participation according to Milbank sufficiently account for the embodiment of participation? Milbank's move to augment the ancient account of participation (as being and knowing) with participation in terms of human making intends to secure just such an emphasis on participation's practical embodiment, grounded in his christological poetics. So the answer to this first question in many ways depends on the answer to this second question: Is Milbank's Jesus embodied and particular enough to ground creation's participation in God or does it tend toward docetism, so that his understanding of human making as participation could stand without its christological ground? I suggest that Milbank's account of participation attends insufficiently to embodiment because it does not begin with the particular embodiment of Jesus and the embodied practices of the church.

An Insufficiently Embodied Participation?

At the very center of *The Word Made Strange* is an important christological essay for understanding the questions raised above, "A Christological Poetics."[12] A close look at this essay will reveal much about Milbank's understanding of participation, for it takes up quite explicitly the question of human making, which, as we have seen, is integral to Milbank's understanding of participation and is in fact what makes his position so

---

clearly how accounts of participation can be given without any christological specification.

12. Milbank, *Word Made Strange*, 123–44.

unique. Indeed, the first several pages outline what he calls a poetics of humanity. Milbank argues that humanity is a "fundamentally poetic being,"[13] meaning at once that humans are makers and that what we make, our poetic products, both carry to some extent our life and intention, the very meaning they are endowed with because our making them is *ours*, but also that their meaning always exceeds our intention so that humans are always confronted by their products as something that addresses them, so to speak.[14] He writes that "to *act at* all is always to be dispossessed, always continuously to apprehend 'more' in our own deed once it 'occurs' to us, than our first hazy probings towards the formulation of a performance could ever have expected."[15] It is this process that is constitutive of our humanity: "In this activity he becomes human."[16] In this assertion of a discovery of "more" in our products, Milbank's account of the human poetic tends toward the theological, a necessary move because this is the realm the so-called secular social sciences try to secure as pure immanence in order to maintain their integrity, as he argues in *Theology and Social Theory*. His account here turns quickly and explicitly theological when he suggests that our openness to the otherness of our own and others' products is an openness to receive grace. This is so precisely because the "more" to our deeds is grounded in the transcendent "more" of their participation in God, a "more" that is always gift. So, as we receive that more from our own products, their irreducible otherness to us their makers, we are open to God's own graciousness. He writes: "To be open to the reception of grace in a preparedness to act, is, therefore, to be open to the risk that another may immediately ruin the gracious character of our 'poetic' performance. But even that formulation is inadequate, for without the 'good' reception by the other, or by many others, we should never in the first place receive at all the grace that is our own act: grace is always humanly mediated both before and 'after' its occurrence."[17] This understanding of the gracious nature of human production and reception, an account that understands also the possibility "of sinful distortion—for which one is both responsible and not responsible—within every action"

13. Ibid., 124.
14. Ibid., 125.
15. Ibid.
16. Ibid.
17. Ibid., 126.

elicits my first worry with Milbank's account of participation.[18] Even while this understanding of human activity is grounded theologically, it has universalized grace as openness and receptivity to the poetic act of another prior to any christological specification. This is not Milbank's last word on the subject, for he moves from the poetics of humanity to a discussion of humanity's "poetic" encounter with God as narrated in the Old Testament, and then to specifically christological speculations. Beginning, however, with a generalized account of humanity's graced poetic, based on a pre-christological account of participation, even if not un-christological in the end, suggests a foundational account that does not need the particularity of Jesus' embodiment to make theological sense of humanity's capacity to make.

This account of the human poetic is foundational in two other senses. First, it provides a foundation as he moves to an explicit description of how God (and not just grace) confronts us:

> The created natural order shows God to us, to be sure, but there is only a conscious awareness of God if he stands "ahead of us" in the realm of "objective spirit" that is human culture. This does *not* mean that God is the immanent process of human understanding, because that conception is ultimately indistinguishable from the idea that God is a pure projection.... Rather it means that because our cultural products confront us and are not truly "in our control" or even "our gift," this allows that somewhere among them God of his own free will finds the space to confront us also.[19]

Here a phenomenology of human culture is foundational for an account of how God confronts humanity through human culture. Furthermore, by drawing on the notion of the noncompetitive relationship between divine and human activity, Milbank extends the above to give an account of how revelation occurs through human culture:

> The event of revelation itself may be defined as the intersection of the divine and human creations. By this is meant that the "overtaking" by the product of the creative act that brings it forth is now seen as the occasion on which God interposes without in any way violating the range of the natural human intent. At the point where the Divine creation establishes the human creation by overtaking and completing it, thereby exposing a realized

18. Ibid., 127.
19. Ibid., 130.

intention more primitive than the human intent and fully its master, there is revelation.[20]

For Milbank, the Exodus becomes an example of just such a revelatory overtaking.

Second, his account of human making becomes hermeneutically foundational as he tries to offer an account of the revelatory significance of the Old Testament. In offering an account of original sin, Milbank writes that "since once a sinful *inhibition* of poetic reception has occurred anywhere, *all* reception is distorted, and we all become responsible for acts and representations not entirely our own. Here, the construal of human activity as 'poetic' allows us to see that the *only* sin is original sin, and that Israel alone located sin by discovering itself to be in an impossible quest for the right *figura*, the right 'poetic boundary of representation.'"[21] What matters here is not what he says about sin, but how he uses his previous account of human poetic activity as a hermeneutic to understand the relationship between God and Israel in the Old Testament. This is done, furthermore, without any attention to particular texts from the Old Testament. Thus the reliance upon what I have called a pre-christological account of humanity's participation in grace through its capacity to make and receive is used here as a hermeneutic to interpret the Old Testament. This, combined with a worrisome neglect of the particularity of the Old Testament text itself, suggests, though I understand does not show definitively, a theological deficiency.

The situation gets more complicated when Milbank turns explicitly to christological concerns, when he asks, "[W]hat difference does Christ make to this picture? In the first place, what light does the figure of Christ in the Gospels throw upon the cunning of poetic reason doubled by the divine command of our intent?"[22] In other words, given the pre-christological account of human making and its relationship to God's own action, what does Jesus have to do with any of this?[23] The very asking of this christological question suggests his earlier speculations are not his last word on the subject.

20. Ibid., 130–31.

21. Ibid., 132.

22. Ibid., 134.

23. The theological method here has the form, if not necessarily the substance, of correlationism.

Milbank's Christology in this essay is an answer to an anthropological question. Having used his account of the poetic of humanity, as we saw above, to offer an understanding of sin, here Milbank offers a restatement of the problem of the human poetic and the divine intent in linguistic terms:

> The entire problematic of the divine overtaking of human purpose in the Old Testament points to the coincidence of the divine presence with the human *telos*. In the first place, humanity as poetic being can have no bounds set to his nature; its only adequate, but unimaginable representation, must be identical with the representation that God always makes of himself. The divine reality and the human end which defines human nature do eternally coincide, because God in his being is an infinity of promise for man. In the second place, humanity's fallenness is defined as an inability to inaugurate a response to the realization of this promise, a collapse of the means of representation, together with the loss of the possibility of a non-tragic ecstatically sundered "responsibility." Humanity's salvation now demands the fully original divine initiative amongst us; this initiative is adequate because it has established a final representation in the incarnate *Logos*, and because it is adequate, it is ontologically unfailing.[24]

Thus Jesus is the answer to this Old Testament problem of representation:

> It is as this divine-human person, who has both finitely and infinitely the character of a representation, that we finally recognize in Jesus the divine overtaking and fulfilling of all human purposes. As the divine utterance, Jesus is the absolute origination of all meaning, but as human utterance Jesus is inheritor of all already constituted human meanings. He is a single utterance in his unified fulfillment of these meanings, such that he becomes the adequate metaphoric representation of the total human intent.[25]

As an interpretation of the salvific effect of the incarnation, this metaphoric-representational model lacks fleshly particularity. Throughout *The Word Made Strange* but especially in this essay, Milbank uses the word *figura* for Jesus. What work does that do? How does it pick Jesus out? How does it identify him? I suspect that speaking of the *figura* of Jesus

24. Milbank, *Word Made Strange*, 135.
25. Ibid., 136.

does two things: It universalizes him *at the expense of his particularity,* and it evacuates the necessity of flesh, for, unfortunately, this linguistic re-interpretation, unlike McCabe's, does not begin with the fundamental bodiliness of language.

That Christ as *figura,* and therefore, for Milbank, that Christ as Savior, is evacuated both of particularity and embodiment is clear in two places: his interpretation of the atonement, and his interpretation of our participation in Christ. As he writes of the cross:

> In the conjuncture of this metonymic death-sign matrix with the fundamentally *metaphoric* character of the sign, we discover the key to the atonement. *Every* sign is a substitution and a representation because it categorically involves the being of one thing—a particular form—only as a relations to other things. In Jesus's metonymic fulfillment of his metaphoric sign character on the Cross, this substitution of himself for all humanity assumes a tragic aspect.[26]

Indeed, Milbank goes on from here to suggest that "Jesus assumes the burden of these false meanings in a perfectly ordinary human way, in that he is directly and personally abused."[27] His non-violent response to this abuse, according to Milbank, allows him to transfigure the "ugly constructions" of this abuse by incorporating them into the context of his life.[28] And here is the reason I said my questions of Milbank's work were not definitive: because this turn to the non-violent particularity of Jesus's response suggests just the sort of focus on Jesus (rather than the *figura* Christ) that upholds particularity and embodiment. Nonetheless, the "abuse" that Jesus suffers here is itself the symbolic, metaphorical representation of the accumulated historical failures of meaning of all humanity. Thus the leather of the whips and the wood of the cross are absorbed by their metaphoric character, and so, potentially, is the flesh of the one so abused.[29]

---

26. Ibid., 139.

27. Ibid.

28. Ibid.

29. For a similar critique of Milbank, see Reno, *In the Ruins of the Church,* 63–79. He writes, "Time and again, Radical Orthodoxy blocks any center of gravity from acquiring weight sufficient to control or direct our participation in God. For example, when Milbank engages the biblical text, he consistently translates the particular sense into a conceptual or speculative process. The Gospel stories are for him allegories of a participa-

It is in his interpretation of our participation in this work that is
"the true fulfillment of Creation in the realm of human work" by looking
at Mary that Milbank explicitly states the un-embodied character of his
linguistic reinterpretation of Christ's work and our discipleship:

> Because Christ's person is present only in and through his work,
> this means that it is present in the relations that he enters into with
> other people and the things of this world; it even has its origin in
> the assent of his mother Mary to the adequate human representa-
> tion. Her assent both grows with the unfolding of the representa-
> tion from its divine conception in her womb and is also, with the
> whole pre-history of Isreal, constitutive of that representation it-
> self. We stand within the *locus* of the Holy Spirit as the area already
> given its horizon by the active assent of Mary. Within this space,
> but to a more restricted degree, our assents to, and fulfillments of,
> Christ's intentions, realize his true relation to us and belong among
> Christ's own proper words. In this way, as that medieval tradition
> summed up in Eckhart has it, Christ the *Logos* is conceived again
> in us—though this may now be understood in more directly lin-
> guistic fashion. It is in this sense of continuing to form the image
> of Christ that we genuinely participate in Christ and not as a kind
> of sub-personal, quasi-material inclusion.[30]

When Milbank suggests that "our assents to, and fulfillments of, Christ's
intentions, realize his true relation to us and belong among Christ's own
proper words," Milbank seems to be expressing an account of participation in Christ that I have been trying to offer ecclesiologically, in which
the church's practices become Christ's own practices as they embody that
shape of participation in the world, a shape discerned by careful attention to the shape of Jesus as presented in the Gospels. Discipleship, so
important for both McCabe and Bonhoeffer, is given its grounding in a
metaphysics of participation so that, through the activities of the disciples
as church, Christ's word and work is embodied in the world. But such
a promising account of embodied participation seems undone with his
explicit remark that the fully linguistic reinterpretation of the atonement

---

tory metaphysics.... The same implicit repudiation of authoritative particularity occurs
when Milbank identifies the church as a process rather than as a tradition of first-order
language and practice.... Whether the focus rests on Scripture, creed, or tradition, a
certain 'ideality' seems to govern, a tendency to think theologically in terms of higher,
purified, and unattained forms" (72).

30. Milbank, *Word Made Strange*, 140–41.

and discipleship is other than a "quasi-material inclusion." Whatever Milbank intends by "sub-personal, quasi-material inclusion," it at least suggests an understanding of language that allows our participation in Christ, the Word, to be something other than our bodily participation through the embodied practices of the church. If this is the case, then his Christology seems, as least from this essay (once again, I don't want to speak for the whole scope of his work) to undermine the very materiality that Radical Orthodoxy as a movement seems to fetishize.

This critique of Milbank's understanding of participation is by no means definitive. He has perhaps done more than any other to make this topic critical once again in theological conversation and has in many ways opened the possibility for the very argument I wish to make. His critique of Platonic participation, even if he is deeply indebted to Plato, opens the way for an understanding of cultural practices to be included in participation and for the Christian distinction between Creator and creation to be incorporated into the account through the *analogia entis*. But when we turn to Milbank's Christology and to his absent ecclesiology he can be read to subvert the positive claims of his earlier accounts of participation. For his Christology, at least in this area, is the answer to a problem about participation, when, it seems, that participation in God in which all human making participates can be understood largely independently of Christ's and the church's own participation in God's life, through which, as I understand it, human making in general finds its participatory *telos* and thus can be said to participate at all. Furthermore, his account of Christ in this and the subsequent essay "The Name of Jesus"[31] presents a linguistic reinterpretation of Jesus without sufficient attention to the particularities of the Jesus of the Gospels; thus his Christology, at least potentially, ignores the significance of the particularity of Jesus (and consequently of the church as an embodied community of discipleship) for his account of participation.

Robert Jenson's Ecclesial Participation

In many ways Jenson stands in stark contrast to Milbank both in terms of method and constructive proposals. I use Jenson here as a contrast to Milbank and as a picture of the possibility—and an argument for the necessity—of an account of the church and of participation that *begins* with

31. Milbank, *Word Made Strange*, 145–68.

the particularity of God's embodiment in the man Jesus and his body, the church, before it can account for creation's participation in general. If Milbank talks of materiality and the materiality of human practices, but potentially fails to ground that materiality in the materiality of Christ and his church, Jenson makes embodiment a theological necessity, for only as bodily and available can the church be Christ for the world.

The heart of Jenson's doctrine of the church is that the church is the *totus Christus*, the whole Christ, participating in God's life as an anticipation of all creation's eschatological participation. In his account of Jesus's and the church's participation in God's life, Jenson makes theological moves that are important for the argument of this book, for— without denying the distinction between creation and Creator, without denying the embodiment of the church, without being beholden to an antecedent metaphysics, and without offering an inadequately Trinitarian account[32]—Jenson argues that as "the church speaks and hears the gospel

32. The first volume of Jenson's systematic theology, *Triune God*, is in many ways a defense of the particularity of the story of God's material identification with the story of human history over against theology that is any way dependent on what I have called an antecedent metaphysics. In this, of course, Jenson takes Barth as his model and inspiration. He writes, "It is a particular and particularly baneful instance of an error earlier noted that theology, when it has acknowledged its own claim to universal scope, has sometimes nevertheless thought it must achieve this by finding 'the right' metaphysics among those offered by officially designated philosophers. . . . The great [counter] example in the twentieth century is the *Kirchliche Dogmatik* of Karl Barth. Barth did not declare independence from 'the philosophers' because philosophy is something so different from theology it must be kept at arm's length. His reason was exactly the opposite: he refused to depend on the official philosophers because what they offered to do for him he thought he should do for himself in conversation with them when that seemed likely to help. The *Kirchliche Dogmatik* is an enormous attempt to interpret all reality by the fact of Christ; indeed, it can be read as the first truly major system of Western metaphysics since the collapse of Hegelianism" (21). So what of Greek philosophy and the question of "being"? Jenson writes, "'Being' is not a biblical concept, or one with which Christian theology must necessarily have been involved, had the gospel's history been different than it is. If we could abstract from actual history, we could, of the biblical God, say 'God is good' and 'God is just' and continue with such propositions at need, without making an issue of the 'is.' And the teaching that God is one could remain the simple denial that anyone but JHWH is God. But 'being' was a central concept of the theology with which the gospel came into essential conversation in Mediterranean antiquity. Thus the concept has become an inextricable determinant of the actual Christian doctrine of God" (207). It is true, for Jenson, that we cannot now avoid speaking of the Christian God with the language of "being," but the truth of this fact is based upon a historical contingency. There is nothing in the gospel itself that requires the use of western metaphysical concepts besides the contingent history of the gospel's penetration of Mediterranean culture.

and as the church responds in prayer and confession, the church's life is a great conversation, and this conversation is none other than our participation in the converse of the Father and the Son in the Spirit."[33] It is in the church's *activity*, for Jenson, or as I would say, in its practicing its life, that the church finds itself practicing the eternal practice of the triune life. This is possible, according to Jenson, precisely because the church is Christ's embodiment in and for the world. Why this participation in the converse that is the life of God must be accounted for christologically is the answer to his own question:

> Father, Son, and Spirit are persons whose communal life is God. Can they indeed bring other persons into that life, as we have in previous chapters often supposed? If the bringing of other persons into the triune life were in such fashion as to "deify" them as to increase the number of persons *whose* life it is, if it added to the identities of God, then God could not accommodate them without undoing himself.[34]

But it is the case that,

> God can indeed, if he chooses, accommodate other persons in his life without distorting that life. God, to state it as boldly as possible, is *roomy*. Indeed, if we were to list divine attributes, roominess would have to come next after jealousy. He can, if he chooses, distinguish himself from others not by excluding them but by including them.[35]

That inclusion is our participation in the life of God. The rest of this section shows the contours of Jenson's account of that participation, that inclusion, that divine attribute he calls roominess.

Milbank is more likely to argue that, while a contingency, this is a necessary contingency for the truthful speaking of God. John Howard Yoder argues, in a way similar to Jenson, that the missionary imperative required a rendering of the Christian gospel in Greek language, even if the gospel must break, so to speak, the rules of the language to allow for the particularity of the gospel message. But Yoder would say we are no longer beholden to the language derived from the missionary effort in Mediterranean antiquity, but rather are compelled in our own context to speak, in whatever language available, the truth that Jesus is Lord and Messiah. Yoder, *Priestly Kingdom*, 46–62.

33. Jenson, *Triune God*, 228.

34. Ibid., 226.

35. Ibid.

AN ECCLESIAL ACCOUNT OF PARTICIPATION

When Jenson turns to a discussion of the church in the second volume of his systematic theology he does so having already spoken of the church several times in the first volume. Indeed, much of what he says in the second volume is an elaboration of briefer accounts of the church given in the first. While the first volume is devoted to the identity of the triune God, that account of the identity of God could not have been given without accounting for the hope of Israel and the role of the community of Israel in the activity of God's enacting his life precisely because, for Jenson, "God's story is committed as a story with creatures. And so he too, as it is, can have no identity except as he meets the temporal end toward which creatures live."[36] Jenson's understanding of the church's participation in God's life begins with Israel's anticipated participation in God's life as that community in creation with whom God's identity is linked. For, as Jenson writes, "The *content* of Israel's fully eschatological hope is, inexorably, hope for participation in God's own reality, for what the Greek fathers of the church called 'deification.' But such a thing cannot be said within Israel's canonical Scripture: until a Resurrection, hope for deification would be intolerable hubris."[37] He continues: "Yes we can already see how this ultimate fulfillment of Israel's hope is to be understood. If God is a God identified by and with the events of Israel's history, Israel's 'deification' will be simply that the corresponding relations on our part are realized, that we come to be identified by and with events in the life of God."[38] Our identification with the events in God's life happens through our incorporation into the body of Jesus who relates to God according to the same structure as Israel. In his resurrection, Jesus is the eschatological fulfillment of Israel's hope to be included in the life of God. Importantly it is in a discussion of the relationship between Israel and Jesus and the relationship between Jesus and God that Jenson locates the importance of the distinction between Creator and created, and not in an antecedent metaphysical speculation; this distinction is disclosed precisely in the drama of God's identification with a created community and with One in that created community who stands in their midst as God himself. Jenson writes,

36. Ibid., 65.
37. Ibid., 71.
38. Ibid., 71.

What these phenomena disclose is what must happen when Israel's hope becomes fully eschatological, when, that is, it becomes in fact hope for inclusion in the divine life. If Israel is to be a participant of the divine life while the difference between God and the creature is maintained there must be—and here "must" is the right word, precisely with respect to God—a difference between an Israelite who stands over against Israel and the people without whom this one is not himself. There must be the one who in his own person can be an agent in the divine life and the community that in his identity with it is taken into that life. There must be one to face the community for the Father and the community to face the Father with him.

Were there only a singular creature who in his own person was "one of the Trinity," in his instance, the difference between God and creature would simply abolish; but, in that the one person is the one he is only as identified with a community whose members are *not*, in their singular persons, identities of God, the one Israelite's membership in God in fact sustains the difference between God and creature. Were there to be only a homogenous plurality of persons to be taken into the triune life, again, the difference between God and creature would vanish in religious murk; but, in that the community subsists only in that the one is within it, this one is, just so, a unique individual whose reality as "one of the Trinity" does not release a proliferation of divine hypostases.[39]

There are three reasons Jenson's discussion of the relationship between Israel, Jesus, and God is important for understanding his account of participation. First, by locating the hope of participation in the life of Israel with Israel's God, there is no way that Jenson's notion of participation can get "off the ground" so to speak in any abstraction that minimizes the embodiment and particularity of that participation. Second, any account of participation must maintain the distinction between God and the creature; again, for Jenson, this distinction is maintained precisely because of the particularity of the Israelite community and the particularity of the one Israelite, Jesus, who stands in that community both as a member and as God. The narrative of these embodiments itself maintains this crucial distinction. Finally, the discussion of Israel and Jesus opens the way for an account of the church as participating in the divine life; and the church's participation, in the end, cannot be comprehended in abstraction from the eschatological fulfillment of Israel's hope in the resurrection of Jesus.

39. Ibid., 83.

For, as Jenson says, "But when it is seen that Israel's destiny can be fulfilled only by the conclusion of this world's history and the beginning of a new reality, no historical space is left in which the ingathering can occur. By Jesus' Resurrection occurring 'first,' a sort of *hole* opens *in* the event of the End, a space for something like what used to be history, for the church and its mission."[40] That *hole* is the roominess of God's life. To Jenson's discussion of the church's inhabiting that roominess we now turn.

Jenson devotes the first volume of his systematic theology to the doctrine of God, the second to God's works *ad extra*. When he begins his discussion of the church and its founding in the trinitarian act of God, Jenson makes a telling suggestion: "It could be argued," he writes, "that in the system here presented, also ecclesiology belongs in the first volume."[41] It can be argued, Jenson suggests, that a theological account of the church belongs not in a discussion of God's works *ad extra*, but that it belongs rather to the first volume, to a discussion of the acts by which God identifies himself as the God he is, that somehow, in a way different from the rest of creation, the church belongs properly to the life of God. He writes, "There is a difference between the church's place in the gospel and that of the creation as such or even creation taken finally into God. Christ is personally the second identity of God, and the *totus Christus* is Christ with the church; therefore the church is not in the same way an *opus ad extra* as the creation, even when it [the creation] is perfected in God."[42] That the church as the whole Christ lives in the life of God so as to make it an appropriate subject of the doctrine of God itself is exactly what makes Jenson's account of participation so compelling. In the end he locates the church in the works *ad extra*, for, following the tradition, he acknowledges that "though we rely on the church as on the presence of God, we do so just in that the church within herself directs us to a presence of God that is not identical with herself."[43]

The first important thing to note about Jenson's ecclesiology is that he wants to emphasize the fully trinitarian founding of the church. He agrees with Eastern critiques of Western accounts of the church, which say that the West wrongly supposes that when one has said everything one needs

40. Ibid., 85.

41. Jenson, *Works of God*, 167.

42. Ibid., 167.

43. Ibid. We've already noted how Bonhoeffer articulates the church as the presence or availability of Christ to the world without being inappropriately identified with Christ.

to say about Christology, one can say everything one needs to say about the church.[44] Bonhoeffer's christological account of the church was weak just insofar as it could not account for the particular and robust activity of the Spirit in the church beyond the claim that the Spirit "actualizes" the church. For Jenson this and any other less than trinitarian account of the church would be inadequate. In his discussion of the founding of the church from perspective of the Father (always remembering that all of the acts of God are acts of the whole Trinity) he places his discussion of election. God wills the church by delaying the parousia and thus making the church an "event *within the event* of the new age's advent."[45] In that delay the election of the Father becomes visible: "The unmediated and wholly antecedent will that is the Father dictates that there be the church, as something other than the world or the Kingdom, and that this church be exactly the one that exists."[46] Most importantly, for out purposes here, is to see how the church's participation in God's life is constitutive of the Father's willing. Jenson writes that "the one sole object of election is Jesus with his people, the *totus Christus*. . . . That it is the man Jesus who is the Son is an event of decision in God; and that the church, with the very individuals who belong to the church, is the body of this person is the *same* event of decision."[47] The Spirit's role in the founding of the church is analogous to the Spirit's activity as the third identity of God as Jenson articulated in volume one. If there the Spirit is the one who frees the Son for the Father and the Father for the Son, then here "the Spirit *frees* an actual human community from merely historical determinisms, to be apt to be united with the Son and thus to be the gateway of creation's translation into God."[48] How Jenson here specifies the role of the Spirit is important, for the Spirit does not free the church from history, but from "merely historical determinisms." He does not make the church some-thing other than an actual human community; the Spirit is not added to the church so that the church can be united to Christ *despite* the actual humanity of the church and its institutional structures and the practices by which the community exists as a community. For "since the church is

44. Ibid., 179.
45. Ibid., 171.
46. Ibid., 173.
47. Ibid., 175.
48. Ibid., 179.

a community within created time, the qualification of the church to be united with the risen Christ must be a qualification of the institutions by which she perdures in time."[49] In other words, it is the Spirit's freeing an actual human community, created and existing in time, embodied in its structures and social practices, that secures the church's *embodiment* as it exists in time as Christ's body in anticipation of the end. Finally, Jenson turns to the role of the Son in the founding of the church. Jenson sees the founding of the church in the whole life of the Son: "For it is the Son's whole life, from his conception by the Holy Spirit to his Ascension, that in fact founds the church."[50] "Christ, we may say, delayed the Parousia by living the story he did and so by being the human person he is, who if he rose to be Lord could not lack just such community as is the church."[51] For Jenson, the church's founding is fully a trinitarian act, and it is that act, at once a decision, a liberation, and a life, that creates the church as just the kind of community it is, actual, historical, embodied, and participating in the life of God.

There is one other aspect, the most important aspect, of Jenson's account of participation. At the heart of Jenson's ecclesiology is his concurrence with the ecumenical proposals that go by the term *communio* ecclesiology, a term emphasizing the fact that the church is a great communion with God and with one another through Christ. His whole account of the church is an engagement with twentieth-century ecclesiology as it has taken shape in ecumenical discussions. But here, in his discussion of communion, which is appropriately a discussion of the church and the Eucharist, Jenson's account of participation is the clearest, for here we find, as we found in Bonhoeffer, identification between Christ and the church.

Interestingly, the subject is broached and discussed in volume one when Jenson turns to the resurrection of Jesus' body. "Jesus' Resurrection as confessed by the church is a *bodily* resurrection, with or without an emptying of the tomb. Somehow there now exists a body that is the living Jesus's human body."[52] For most of Christian history, within the Ptolemaic cosmology, this body was considered to be in heaven. But for Jenson, heaven is both the "created future's presence to God . . . [and] also the cre-

---

49. Ibid., 182.
50. Ibid., 183.
51. Ibid.
52. Jenson, *Triune God*, 201.

ated place for the presence of God."[53] After the collapse of the Ptolemaic cosmology, however, there did not seem to be a place for the risen body, and without a place, how can it be a "body" at all? This is the question that animates Jenson's discussion of the church and the Eucharist. Jenson's answer is simple and important. The "entity rightly called the body of Christ is whatever object it is that is Christ's availability to us as subjects; by the promise of Christ, this object is the bread and cup and the gathering of the church around them. *There* is where creatures can locate him, to respond to his word to them."[54] Jenson makes this claim on the basis of his rejection of a perceived ontological inhibition inherited from Western metaphysics, an inhibition Paul himself did not possess in regard to understanding what it means to be "body." Jenson writes of Paul's understanding of body:

> In Paul's language, someone's "body" is simply the person him or herself insofar as this person is *available* to other persons and to him or herself, insofar as the person is an *object* for other persons and him or herself.... In Paul's ontology, such personal availability may or may not be constituted as the biological entity moderns first think of as "a body"; for Paul, a "spiritual" body, whatever that may be, is as much or more a body as is a biological body.[55]

This is precisely why when Jenson discusses the church as the body of Christ, he rejects the unhelpful but perennially employed notion of the invisible church. "The concept of the invisible church has occasioned little but trouble throughout theological history, and no use will be made of it in this work. The church is not an invisible entity; she is the, if anything, all too visible gathering of sinners around a loaf and cup."[56] And she must be visible if the church around a loaf and cup is that object which the subject Christ looks to as his own availability to himself and his availability to the world. Whatever it means to say that the church is Christ's body, it must be

---

53. Ibid.

54. Ibid., 205.

55. Ibid. This is almost identical to the claims we have already seen Herbert McCabe makes about "body" as communication or availability. McCabe, discussing Jesus, said that Jesus is more bodily after the resurrection precisely because his availability as body no longer implied his absence.

56. Jenson, *Works of God*, 174. Thus, as Jenson takes up the ecumenically dominant *communio* ecclesiology, by denying the dichotomy visible/invisible, Jenson's account is not troubled by the traditional dichotomies which have already been critiqued.

that this body can be *seen* if it is to be Christ's availability to the world. So while "body" for Jenson does not necessarily imply the biological entity we know as a body, it is always *embodied*, for only as embodied is a "body" available. The church as Christ's body is supremely *embodied*, in that as the church Christ is *more* available than when he walked the earth around 30 AD.

How is the church's embodied participation in Christ, as the community gathered around a loaf and cup that is Christ's availability to the community, to be understood? Jenson, once again critiquing the way Western metaphysics has been employed to make sense of these ontological and sacramental questions, does not resort, nor does he think he needs to resort, to any of the classical metaphysical questions surrounding the presence and absence of Christ in the Eucharist or the church. Rather, he adverts simply to the fact that Christ, as the *Logos*, that is, as the first and last determinant of reality, deems the loaf and the cup and the gathered community to be his availability to himself and to the world. He writes,

> No metaphor or ontological evasion should be intended. Sacrament and church are *truly* Christ's body for us, because Christ himself takes these same things for the object as which he is available to himself. For the proposition that the church is a human body of the risen Jesus to be ontically and straightforwardly true, all that is required is that Jesus indeed be the Logos of God, so that his self-understanding determines what is real.[57]

Thus he concludes his discussion of the embodiment of Christ in the world in the first volume:

> The subject that the risen Christ is, is the subject who comes to word in the gospel. The object—the body—that the risen Christ is, is the body in the world to which this word calls our intention, the church around her sacrament. He needs no other body to be a risen man, body and soul. There is and needs to be no other place than the church for him to be embodied, nor in that other place any other entity to be the "real" body of Christ. Heaven is where God takes space in his creation to be present to the whole of it; he does that in the church.[58]

57. Jenson, *Triune God*, 206.
58. Ibid.

We are beginning to see the nature of participation for Jenson. As the body of Christ, the church is God's space in the world to be available to the world. The church's participation in the life of God is not for the church's benefit alone, but it's constitutive of the church's mission in the world just as the church is constitutive of God's mission in the world. The "by and with" identification of God with Israel has achieved realization in the community of the church just insofar as the church is the present yet anticipated participation of the community in the very life of God even as it continues to await the fullness of the End when all creation will be translated into God's life. The church's participation in God's life through Christ and the Spirit is, as a firstfruits, the gateway for the rest of creation's participation. Rather than positing creation's participation in God *qua* creation using the categories of a received metaphysics, Jenson is clear that creation's participation is teleological and particular, teleological in that creation awaits its participation in God's life, and particular because that participation will be through the church's participation, which is the particular community made apt by the Spirit to be united to the Son for no other reason than that the Father wills it. Jenson's account of participation can be appropriately summarized with his own words:

> The church, we have said, exists by anticipation. What she antici-
> pates is inclusion in the triune communion. In the End, the *koi-*
> *nonia* that the risen Christ and his Father now live in their Spirit
> will become the mutual love in which believers will limitlessly
> find one another. The church exists to become that fellowship; the
> church's own communal Spirit is sheer *arrabon* of that Community.
> Thus the church's present reality anticipates, in all brokenness and
> fallibility, the end of all things, exactly as the end is the Trinity's
> embrace of "all in all." We may say: *the communion that is now the*
> *church is itself constituted by an event of communion or participa-*
> *tion, with the communion that is the Trinity.*[59]

That participation is the church's embodied participation in the life of God as Christ's embodiment, practicing his availability in the world.

Milbank and Jenson present two pictures of participation, at once similar in certain concerns, but significantly different in the end. More specifically, Milbank's focus on materiality can tend toward ideality just insofar as his Jesus loses his particular embodiment when he becomes reinterpreted linguistically and universalized. Jenson, on the other hand,

---

59. Jenson, *Works of God*, 222; emphasis added.

understands the church in its materiality as precisely that body which participates in the life of God as the body of the man Jesus. God's "roominess" is the result of God's decision to identify himself by and with the events in the life of Israel, Jesus, and the church in all their embodied particularity. Furthermore, Milbank and Jenson differ methodologically insofar as Milbank can give pre-Christological accounts of creation *qua* creation's (which includes the full range of human cultural making) participation in God, while Jenson can only speak of creation's participation in God as a result of the particular participation of the church in God's life. Thus, an account of the church's embodied participation in the life of God as the gateway to creation's participation in God's life will look more like Jenson's than Milbank's, if the concern for the embodiment and particularity of the church is of crucial importance, as I think it is. Now we turn to the third variety of participation whose account stands between Milbank and Jenson in a way. Norman Wirzba, as we will see, stands with Jenson in his acknowledgment of the particular embodiment of our participation in God and God's activity, but stands closer to Milbank in that he justifies this, not through the particularities of the man Jesus's own embodiment of the life of God, but of a prior and general understanding of the sacramentality of all creation.

Norman Wirzba and the Sacramentality of Creation

Norman Wirzba, an agrarian philosopher and advocate for local economies and sustainable agriculture, has produced in *The Paradise of God: Renewing Religion in an Ecological Age* an unlikely but important work for the retrieval of an embodied account of participation in God's life. He begins, however, not from the perspective of the church, though he has some interesting things to say about the church, but from the perspective of creation and responsible agrarian practice. Importantly, though, Wirzba does not divorce redemption from creation, as if redemption were an afterthought, but offers an account of creation as always already headed toward redemption:

> When we link the work of creation to the work of redemption, we are enabled to see that creation, rather than being a static achievement completed in the past, is the dynamic arena in which God's love and peace are working themselves out. Redemption or salvation is not something that is added to an otherwise fully

formed work—it is not an afterthought of God, prompted by the realization that something has gone wrong. Instead the act of creating is itself already an indication of what God ordains as a complete life.[60]

This refusal to divorce redemption from his account of creation is important precisely because, for Wirzba, "In creating the world, God opens a space in which we are invited to participate in the joy of the divine life."[61] So in the very act of creating, God intends for the creation to share in God's own life; this sharing is both the beginning and the end of the creation, in that it is God's original intent and the outcome of salvation. "The work of redemption, in this case, would refer to the restoration of the space of creation so that all of creation can once again share in the fullness of the life that God is."[62]

This notion of God's creation participating in God's life is an important aspect of Wirzba's ecological account of creation. As we live in God's creation we serve, humbly and hospitably as "God's agents called to participate in the redemption of a suffering creation."[63] Wirzba argues that in modernity humanity lost its sense of at-homeness in the world as God's creation. Creation became objectified and instrumental, no longer that which God has called to share in God's own life. Thus, by offering an account of creation-redemption which takes with full seriousness the story of God's salvation in Christ, Wirzba is able to articulate a sense of humanity's place in creation as both fully created but also with the unique vocation to join God in the work of creation-redemption. As he says, "human beings are set apart from creation not because they are *other than* creation but because they have a unique role to play *within* creation."[64] Only when humanity's unique vocation within creation is understood, that vocation to become students and servants of God's creation, can humanity find, or recover, its way into the life of God. "As we become the servants of creation," Wirzba writes, "we participate in God's own creative life, fulfill our true vocation, and enjoy more deeply the glory of creation, the paradise

---

60. Wirzba, *Paradise*, 18.

61. Ibid., 19. For Jenson, the space in God's life is created not by God's act of creation by the resurrection, which is also the door, so to speak, through which the rest of creation shares in God's life.

62. Ibid., 19.

63. Ibid., 18.

64. Ibid., 127.

of God."[65] Wirzba's account of creation as moving toward redemption allows him to articulate a convincing account of humanity's unique role in creation as servants and students of creation; and this posture of humility before the rest of creation makes humans co-sharers with God in God's creative and redemptive activity, and thus participants in God's own life. He writes that "the work of humanity consists in the hospitable gesture of welcoming and enabling the whole creation to share in the peace and joy of the divine life."[66]

Wirzba's picture of participation is appealing for two particular reasons. First, his notion of participation is thoroughly embodied. "To know this God, as contrasted with the God of the philosophers, is to enter into God's intention, which means a participation in the movement of the divine life."[67] But that entering into God's intention is not, as in modernity, to enter into piety in an individual, interior way, nor is it to accept the doctrines or beliefs with the mind alone. In modernity, Wirzba argues, "Religion as a set of practical dispositions is eclipsed by religion as a set of ideas or doctrines. All of this is to say that the mind of the self, rather than the activity of a social group, comes to determine the way religion is understood. Religion becomes a more abstract affair, separated from the daily habits of its followers."[68] The relationship between this account of religion and my argument about ecclesiology should be clear: the heart of the church is not its abstract, ideational center, related somehow to God; the church is constituted by particular embodied practices. Thus the second reason his account is worthwhile is that participation for him is an *activity*; it is not in the static being of what is created. Wirzba recognizes that creation itself is a teleological concept and our participation in God's life is embodied in teleological practices. For Wirzba, to enter into God's intention, and thus into God's life, is to fulfill humanity's vocation to be students and servants of creation as that is embodied in particular practices, indeed in the embodied "hospitable gesture of welcoming" creation to share in God's life.

· 65. Ibid., 148.

66. Ibid., 21.

67. Ibid., 71.

68. Ibid.

There is one particular hospitable gesture of welcoming that Wirzba upholds over and over again as an important practice in which humans share the divine life:

> When God created the earth, God "made room" for us all and in so doing showed us that the heart of the divine life, indeed all life, is this generous and gracious gesture. As we garden, that is, as we weed out the nonnurturing elements within us and train our habits to be more life promoting, we participate in the divine life and learn to see and feel the creation as God sees and feels it.[69]

And again:

> Work, rather than following from divine punishment, becomes the noble activity of presenting to God a creation strengthened and restored through the exercise of our hands, heart, and head. It is to join with God in the divine work of cultivating and maintaining a garden. It is to enter into the flow of the divine beneficence and hospitality.[70]

And finally:

> If we understand God's creation as "making room" and then also understand that the life that is invited into God's presence comes from and is dependent on the earth, then the destruction of soil is a direct affront to the life and work of God. Restoration of soil, in turn, becomes a primary focus through which we participate in the divine life.[71]

Participation in the life of God is at the heart of Wirzba's theological account of humanity's place in the world. And one of the primary practices through which we participate in God's life is through the practice of gardening and through related practices that put us in careful and respectful contact with the soil, contact that brings life and health to God's earth, rather than harm and destruction. The gesture of cultivating soil is a hospitable and humanizing gesture, a gesture through which humans begin to fulfill their own vocation as participants in God's life and work and through which they welcome the rest of creation into creation's *telos*, into life with God.

69. Ibid., 118.
70. Ibid., 155.
71. Ibid., 21.

The weakness in Wirzba's work is in the account of creation's sacramentality that underlies and justifies his view of working with the soil as participation in the life of God. His most extended account of the sacramentality of all creation is as follows:

> To speak of the sacraments or, more specifically, to participate in a sacramentally defined universe is to live with the insight that the mundane is never simply mundane. Divine grace, though symbolized in the various actions of the church, is understood by a sacramental mind to pervade the whole of reality, since reality, before being an objective datum that exists to be studied and manipulated by a form-giving mind, bears witness to its own gratuitous givenness. On the sacramental view ... the sense of reality as creation is palpable because reality is understood in terms of its graced origin. And God as the creator is known in the very life movements of which God is the source. The character of God, and our ability to enter into the presence of the divine life, is not confined to the words of a scriptural text, but is revealed in the grace of work and play, life and death.[72]

This account of the sacramentality of the world relativizes the particular sacramental practices of the church by understanding them as symbols or intensifications of the world's given sacramentality *qua* creation. It's not wrong to say that the "sense of reality as creation is palpable because reality is understood in terms of its graced origins," but it must be recognized that such graced origins are graced precisely insofar as the origin has in view the end toward which it is moving. Far from symbolizing the sacramentality of the world, in the particular sacramental acts of the church—and in these acts I include both preaching and Eucharistic celebration—creation

---

72. Ibid., 70. This is exactly the account of sacramentality, similar to Milbank's, which both Jenson and Rowan Williams oppose. Jenson writes of the struggle to understand sacramental realities, "The effort [to understand sacramental reality] cannot be to construe an ontological sort on general principles, in order then to classify the church's sacramental events as of that sort. Thus it can be very misleading to speak of a special 'sacramental universe' within which sacraments have their being or of some generally sacramental character of created being, which enables the church's specific sacramental life" (*Works of God*, 250). See also Williams, *On Christian Theology*, 201, 218. He writes, "There is, then, a sacramental practice, something that does indeed reflect on how we see matter in general; but it is not, I think, a 'sacramental principle' enabling us to recognize divine *presence* in all things. It is more that the divine presence is apprehending by seeing in all things their difference, their particularity, their 'not-God-ness,' since we have learned what the divine action is in the renunciation of Christ, his giving himself into inanimate form" (218).

as creation finds its end in the church's embodied practices, and thus can be understood as creation moving toward redemption, a redemption not symbolized but realized sacramentally in the church's embodied practicing of its own life. Before one can see or understand what it means to talk about the sacramentality of creation, one needs to begin with an account of the particular sacramental acts of the church, an account not unlike the one I have given in the previous two chapters. Only when this is the case can we keep the church from being a "representative of Christ on earth" or an "abiding witness and agent" to what God is already doing through the sacramentality of the world in general.[73] This is precisely the reason in this book a discussion of the appropriate way to understand the relationship between God and the world and the world and the church comes at the end—the third guiding question—because adequate accounts of such relations are given in terms of the particularity of Christ's incarnation as it is continued and practiced in the church, rather than in pre-ecclesial accounts of creation and general accounts of sacramentality of which incarnation and sacrament are symbols or intensifications.

I wanted to end the discussion of different versions of participation with a discussion of Wirzba for two reasons. First, he comes, like Jenson, very close to linking participation in the life of God to embodied social practices, to particular human, teleological activities. Second, his account also highlights those particular areas where I think an account of participation needs to be rethought. By blending a general account of religion with the particularities of Christianity, Wirzba admirably ties participation to the particular life of the triune God, but he also gives accounts of non-particular practices, like working with the soil, which have a justification in a general account of creation's sacramentality in a way that reverses what I consider to be the appropriate direction of thought. Without a more dense ecclesiology, from which any account of participation must proceed, it is hard to see how working with the soil, even in careful and hospitable ways, can be understood as participation in the life of God. That is precisely the kind of ecclesiology we saw that Milbank lacked and Jenson provided. Such practices that Wirzba identified indeed can be practices of participation, but only derivatively, only when they find their origin and *telos*, not in the sacramentality of creation *qua* cre-

73. Wirzba, *Paradise*, 48.

ation, but in a sacramental teleology in which creation *becomes* sacrament in the practices of the church.

CONCLUSION

In this discussion of the varieties of participation we can see the beginning outline of what might be called five criteria for an account of participation faithful to the embodied existence of the church in the world:

1. An account of participation must faithfully maintain the distinction between Creator and creature. We saw that Jenson did this in an important way, for that distinction in Jenson became a constitutive element of the narrative of God's identification of himself "by and with" the events of history, particularly the events of the life of Israel, Jesus, and the church. Thus in Jenson this distinction served the purposes of securing the particularity of that which participates in God.

2. An account of participation must be given in terms of the particular and embodied nature of the church. I argued that Milbank, despite Radical Orthodoxy's talk of materiality, failed in certain respects to deliver an embodied participation because he reinterpreted the particularity of Jesus's life in terms of a linguistics insufficiently tied to the body. Jenson and Wirzba on the other hand point to the particularity of creation and the particularity of practices as constitutive elements of their understanding of participation.

3. An account of participation must begin with the particularity of Christ and the church and not in a general account of creation's participation in God *qua* creation. Creation's participation can only be understood teleologically, as a movement toward an ever deepening participation in God through what Jenson calls the gateway of the church. Milbank and Wirzba are both insufficient in this respect, while Jenson is clear, "The effort [in sacramental theology] cannot be to construe an ontological sort on general principles, in order then to classify the church's sacramental events as of that sort. Thus it can be very misleading to speak of a special 'sacramental universe' within which sacraments have their being or of some generally sacramental character of created being

which enables the church's specific sacramental life."[74] This claim is a constitutive element of my understanding of participation.

4. An account of participation should show how participation in God is not an invisible essence or interiority, but is socially visible and has the shape of the life of Jesus's peaceableness. Though this has not been specifically argued in the discussion of participation, it is a point that has been repeatedly made in previous chapters.

5. An account of participation will need to be given in particular terms of the activity of the triune God. This is implied in (2) above.

It's to just such a fully trinitarian account of participation, using the work of Maximus the Confessor, that I now turn.

74. Jenson, *Works of God*, 150.

6

Participation in the Triune God

MAXIMUS THE CONFESSOR, THE great seventh-century theological exponent of Chalcedonian orthodoxy and martyr for the same, is enormously helpful for the argument of this book. He is the last figure I will discuss because I will use his understanding of deification, after I have constructively coupled that with his reflections on the church and the liturgy, to argue for a christological account of participation that justifies and supports my claim that the church is Christ's practicing himself in the Spirit and that such participation in God through Christ has a peculiar visibility that is the church's visible faithfulness in the world. I will look at two texts from Maximus to make my argument. First, I will look at *Ambiguum 7* in which Maximus argues that "Jesus Christ is the substance of virtue."[1] This christological account of deification and the life of virtue will be connected to his account of the church in the *Mystagogia*. Throughout this book, beginning with Cyril of Alexandria in chapter 1, I have argued for the importance of Chalcedonian Christology for any understanding of the embodied church's participation in God's life. As the seventh-century champion of Cyrilline orthodoxy, Maximus makes theological moves that help us to understand the church's participation in God through Christ. He also gives insights into the Holy Spirit's work that will help us to extend this Christology of the church into a fully trinitarian account of the church's participation in the life of God.

VIRTUE AND CHRISTOLOGY IN *AMBIGUUM 7*

Ambiguum 7 presents itself as a point by point refutation of the Origenist notion that all being was originally at rest in God then moved, falling

---

1. Maximus the Confessor, *Ambiguum 7*, 45–74. Citations will be given according to line numbers in this edition.

THE SHAPE OF PARTICIPATION

from that rest into bodies as a kind of punishment. More specifically, it is a refutation of anyone who uses Gregory Nazianzus's work to support such a view. Maximus's work is not a mere refutation, however, for in the course of commenting on Gregory Nazianzus and refuting the Origenists, Maximus displays the major elements of his cosmic teleological vision, his vision of a creation made by the will of God and moving inevitably toward God as toward perfect rest. Moreover, it becomes clear how his thoroughgoing Chalcedonianism is the theological driving force of his cosmic vision, for things "that are by nature separated from one another return to a unity as they converge together in the one human being," that is, Jesus Christ.[2] Maximus's refutation of Origenism entails and illuminates the major themes of his own theological vision, a theological vision that is dogmatically christological and oriented toward the participation of all things in God.

What is less clear, but no less important, is the place a life of virtue plays in Maximus's cosmic christological vision. As part of his argument against Origenism, Maximus makes what looks like a brief digression to discuss virtue, noting that participation in a life of virtue is participation in God. "It is evident," he writes, "that every person who participates in virtue as a matter of habit unquestionably participates in God, the substance of virtues."[3] As he says earlier in the same paragraph, "There can be no doubt that the one Word of God is the substance of virtue in each person. For our Lord Jesus Christ himself is the substance of all the virtues."[4] I will argue that Maximus's account of virtue is a microcosm of his broader overall vision of a creation moving toward union with God in Christ. For Maximus, Chalcedonian Christology and the cosmic vision he unfolds around it is virtue itself. And when this account of virtue is extended to the activity of the church, as I will do in a discussion of the *Mystagogia*, we will see how the church stands at the center of his Christology of participation as the cosmic *telos* of the rest of creation's entry into God.

Let us look first at his brief references to virtue before seeing how his arguments against Origenism entail his account of virtue. There are three things to notice in his brief discussion of virtue. First, clearly shown in the quotations above, the life of virtue is depicted in terms of participa-

2. Ibid., 1092C.
3. Ibid., 1081D.
4. Ibid.

tion. Since the "Word of God is the substance of virtue in each person" then whoever lives a life of virtue participates in God, "the substance of virtues."[5] Later we will have a fuller sense of what "participation" means; here we should just note that virtue is already theologically understood; virtue is presented as a theological, christological category. Second, and more specifically, virtue is not only a way of participating in divinity, it is divinization itself. Maximus argues that the life of virtue is a life that leads toward one's beginning, which is one's true end. The beginning is God from whom we received our being; as we move toward this beginning-as-end in a life of virtue we are conformed to the end so that we not only participate in God in terms of our being, but we become divinized. "As to the end," Maximus writes, "one zealously traverses one's course toward the beginning and source without deviation by means of one's good will and choice. And through this course one becomes God, being made God by God."[6] If the life of virtue is first a life of participation in God, it is furthermore a life of deification in which we are so conformed to God we become God. Maximus is clear, however, that deification never obliterates the distinction between God and creation even if his language of "becoming God" seems to suggest pure identity of essence. He points to this distinction when he says that Christ is the substance of virtue "absolutely, since he is wisdom and righteousness and sanctification itself" whereas these are only attributed to us.[7] The distinction between Christ as the substance of virtue and virtue attributed to humans is an exemplification of a fundamental metaphysical claim about God and creation, a claim he makes a little earlier: "It is impossible for the infinite to exist on the same level of being as the finite things, and no argument will ever be capable of demonstrating that being and what is beyond being are the same."[8] This fundamental claim sets the parameters in which all talk of participation and deification must take place, as we have seen in the first of the five criteria outlined above;[9] participation and deification truly happen, but only in ways appropriate to our existence as creatures; never in a way that

5. Ibid.

6. Ibid., 1084A.

7. Ibid.

8. Ibid., 1081B.

9. This distinction and its corollary, the noncompetitive relationship between divine and human activity, is entailed in Milbank's recovery of the *analogia entis* over against a univocal conception of being in which God and humanity (indeed all creation) share the same playing field, so to speak.

THE SHAPE OF PARTICIPATION

violates our nature by letting us share essentially in divinity. This claim is crucial to understanding the third point: the life of virtue moving toward deification is at once a voluntary life freely chosen and a life given by God. For while "the many are directed toward the One and providentially guided in that direction," the likeness to God that we achieve, that is deification, is "acquired by the practice of virtue and the exercise of the will."[10] These seemingly contradictory claims are made possible by the fundamental metaphysical distinction between God and creation, that what has being and what is beyond being do not share metaphysical space and thus exist in a noncompetitive relationship, so the life of virtue can be at once a life freely practiced by the exercise of the will that moves us toward God-likeness and a life given by God through which we receive deification.

These are the contours of the brief account of virtue Maximus gives in the middle of *Ambiguum 7*. For him virtue is a thoroughly theological category; but this still requires further exemplification. If his explicit account of virtue here seems both short and incomplete, it could only seem thus if we separate it from the rest of his cosmic christological vision. But seen as an integral part of that vision, indeed a microcosm of that vision itself, then it becomes clear that his account of virtue is nothing other than his Chalcedonian Christology conceived in terms of his cosmic vision. We must turn to his arguments against Origenism to see how this is so.

Movement, Well-being, and Deification

Maximus begins his argument against Origenism—a position that says we received bodies as a punishment for our movement away from our original and secure place in God—with his arguments concerning movement.[11] For the Origenist creation is a result of the movement of things preceding their creation; movement, for the Origenists, follows our rest in God and precedes our coming into being. Maximus, in order to refute these claims, must show their incoherence based on an alternative account of movement. For Maximus, movement is always toward some end; thus, if creation is still in movement, as it obviously is, then it has not yet achieved its end, rest. As he writes, "For movement driven by de-

10. Maximus, *Ambiguum 7*, 1084A.
11. Ibid., 1069A.

sire has not yet come to rest in that which is ultimately desirable."[12] The Origenists claim, according to Maximus, that rational beings had already reached their end and subsequently "moved from their secure abode in what is ultimately desirable."[13] If that movement from ultimate rest had happened once, what, he asks, keeps it from happening *ad infinitum*, so that the "secure abode" is not at all secure? Furthermore, he contends that "coming into being precedes movement"[14] because nothing can be and at the same time be unmoved, for that is what it means to be divine, and what comes into being would thus be its own end, which is impossible. Rather, things come into being through God's creating them and they subsequently move toward God, their beginning and final, ultimate place of rest.[15] This movement, Maximus says, "that is tending toward its proper end is called a natural power, or passion, or movement passing from one thing to another and having impassibility as its end."[16] Thus Maximus makes three affirmations about movement from his arguments against the Origenists: First, whatever is moving is moving toward its ultimate end and has not yet achieved it. Second, once ultimate rest has been achieved movement away from it is impossible; thus ultimate rest has never been achieved. Third, coming into being—creation—precedes movement and the movement that follows creation is a natural tending of things towards its beginning—God—which is also its final end.

It will become clear how this account of movement, which is nothing other than a brief statement of Maximus's cosmic teleology without its christological foundations having yet been made explicit, is also his account of virtue, when we see how movement applies to rational beings. First, we should highlight that this movement is a natural inclination of the created thing, an inherent power. All things are moved toward God their end by their inherent power of movement given in God's creating them; thus, God, the first cause, is also the final end. As Maximus writes, "Therefore no creature has ever ceased using his *inherent power* that directs it towards its end, nor has it ceased the *natural activity* that impels it towards its end. . . . *It belongs to creatures* to be moved toward that end

12. Ibid., 1069B.
13. Ibid., 1069C.
14. Ibid., 1072A.
15. Ibid., 1072B.
16. Ibid., 1072B.

which is without beginning, and to come to rest in the perfect end that is without end...."[17] What happens when this account of natural movement, movement that "belongs to creatures," is applied to rational beings?

"If then rational beings come into being, surely they are also moved, since they move from a natural beginning in 'being' toward and voluntary end in 'well-being.'"[18] This "voluntary end," well-being, is not the final end, ultimately desirable rest; rather, it is the name Maximus gives to the movement of rational beings toward their final end in God, for there is an end beyond well-being which is the end of the rational being's movement itself, "eternal well-being." The rational being moves from "being" that is given by God at its beginning, toward and through "well-being" that is at once given by God and a voluntary end of the rational being, to "eternal well-being," our final rest in God. As Maximus writes, "For God is the beginning and the end. From him come both our moving in whatever way from a beginning and our *moving in a certain way* toward him as an end."[19] "Well-being" is just the name for that "moving in a certain way" toward God as the end, a moving that is at once God-given and voluntary.

How can this "moving in a certain way" toward God, "well-being," be given by God and yet be voluntary? Maximus prizes free-will and wants in no way to compromise it. We already noticed above that Maximus's fundamental metaphysical distinction between God and creation puts the movement of rational beings and God in a non-competitive relationship. Here he elaborates, further specifying what he means by the voluntary will being moved by God, when he writes, "That which is in our power, our free will, through which the power of corruption entered into us, will surrender voluntarily to God and will have mastery of itself because it had been taught to refrain from willing anything other than what God wills ... so that from the one from whom we have received being we long to receive being moved as well."[20] This voluntary "being moved" by God is otherwise known as our divinization, so that our will is so closely aligned with God's that Maximus can say it "becomes God" in a way appropriate to it, not compromising its created nature. Nonetheless, this becoming God, the total alignment of the wills, allows Maximus to say that through

17. Ibid., 1073B; emphasis added.
18. Ibid., 1073C.
19. Ibid.; emphasis added.
20. Ibid., 1076B.

"the abundant grace of the Spirit it will be shown that God alone is at work, and in all things there will be only one activity, that of God and of those worthy of kinship with God."[21] The activity of God and of human beings can be referred to as one activity, the activity of God alone, when the wills are so intimately aligned that the human will, moving itself, is also moved by God. This is what Maximus calls "well-being."

Maximus's phrase "the Word of God is the substance of virtue," then, is precisely a shorthand way of giving an account of the movement of rational beings from their beginning in being to "well-being" in which they are voluntarily moved by God and at once participating in God and experiencing deification in a way that does not compromise the distinction between God and the creature. For as Maximus says in his account of virtue, "Whoever by his choices cultivates the good natural seed shows the end to be the same as the beginning and the beginning to be the same as the end."[22] The life of virtue is the voluntary life of conforming the will and being conformed to the will of God, a life of "well-being" given by God and voluntarily enacted, a life that shows the beginning, the first cause from which we proceed, God, to be the end, the final and ultimately desirable resting place from which we will not move. The three principles in Maximus's discussion of virtue outlined above are the three principles of movement of rational creatures in Maximus's cosmic teleological account of creation: participation in God as the beginning of being, voluntary movement toward God that is at the same time a being moved by God, and deification, which is not an end separate from the movement of well-being toward God, but just is the process of that movement and its end. All three of these elements are present in his summarization of his initial discussion of virtue, which also summarizes his entire account of the movement of beings toward God: "As to the beginning, in addition to receiving being itself, one receives natural good by participation: as to the end, one zealously traverses one's course toward the beginning and source without deviation by means of one's good will and choice. And through this course one becomes God, being made God by God."[23] Participation, voluntary movement, and deification—these describe the movement of rational beings from God and to God, outlined in Maximus's initial ar-

21. Ibid., 1076C.
22. Ibid., 1084A.
23. Ibid., 1084A.

guments against the Origenists, and encompassed in the phrase, "There can be no doubt that the Word of God is the substance of virtue in each person."[24]

Portions of God

The Origenists, apparently, took Gregory Nazianzus' phrase "we who are a portion of God"[25] to mean our existence in the One before we fell through movement into our bodies. If in the first section Maximus outlined his cosmic teleology in terms of movement and well-being, here, in order to refute this contention of the Origenists, he gives christological specification to his earlier cosmic teleology to show that our being "portions of God" is a chrstological claim about our beginning and final end and does not refer to a primordial oneness in God that broke apart through movement. With this christological specification it will become even more clear that Maximus's account of virtue is a microcosm of his christological account of creation, his cosmic christological teleology.

Maximus's second major, and more christological, argument against Origenism is essentially an explication of the claim, "the Logos is many *logoi*."[26] These *logoi* are the principles of created things, the principles of the uniqueness of each created thing and of the "incomparable differences among created things."[27] These *logoi* are the Logos, the second person of the Trinity; they inhere in the Logos and pre-exist in the Logos. As Maximus writes, "Because he held together in himself the *logoi* before they came to be, by his gracious will he created things visible and invisible out of non-being."[28] The *logoi* are essentially non-existent principles of things that exist or will exist which inhere in the Logos himself who is the agent of creation. Thus the Logos, the wisdom of God, makes all things that are and that will be in accordance with the principles of the *logoi* that pre-exist together in the eternal Logos. Maximus quotes Ephesians to display this relationship between the Logos, the *logoi*, and the things created in accordance with the principles of the *logoi*, saying, "This same Logos, whose goodness is revealed and multiplied in all things that have

24. Ibid., 1081D.
25. Ibid., 1068D.
26. Ibid., 1077C.
27. Ibid.
28. Ibid., 1080A.

their origin in him, with the degree of beauty appropriate to each be-ing, *recapitulates all things in himself.*[29] The created things are beautiful because each exists in accordance with the principle of its own *logos*, all of which inhere in the divine Logos who brings things into existence from non-being in accordance with those very *logoi*.

This basic account of the relationship between the Logos, *logoi*, and created things is extended in a way that shows how the relationship between the Logos and the *logoi*, this christological account of creation, is the theological rational for Maximus's earlier account of movement, when he writes, "Through this Logos there came to be both being and continuing to be, for from him the things that were made came in a certain way for a certain reason, and by continuing to be and by moving, they participate in God."[30] Maximus's earlier account of movement sub-sequent to coming into being is here given christological specification: Things come to be and continue to be in accordance with the creating Logos who makes things according to the *logoi* that pre-exist in him, things that continue to exist according to these *logoi*. Insofar as things come to be and continue to be, especially rational beings, in accordance with the pre-existent *logoi*, it is appropriate to say that they are "portions of God" by virtue of the *logoi*.

Not only is a rational being a "portion of God" through its creation by the Logos according to its pre-existent *logos*; it also continues to be, moves toward God, by the principle of that same *logos*. That the *logoi* inhere in the Logos is the christological claim that makes sense of participation in God. "Surely, then," Maximus writes, "if someone is moved according to the Logos, he will come to be in God, in whom the *logos* of his being pre-exists as his beginning and cause."[31] The *logos* of each rational creature is the principle by which that creature moves appropriately toward God, its beginning and end. This movement, though in accordance with the *logos* of creation, is nonetheless a striving, a movement of the will toward what is ultimately desirable. In this way, the *logos* of human existence in also the principle of human "well-being" in that it is in accordance with our nature as determined by our *logos* that we move voluntarily in a way that comprises our deification. Thus Maximus: "Rather, by constant straining

29. Ibid., 1080B.
30. Ibid.
31. Ibid., 1080C.

toward God, he becomes God and is called a 'portion of God' because he has become fit to participate in God. By drawing on wisdom and reason and by appropriate movement he lays hold of his beginning and cause."[32] And what is that beginning and cause? It is the Logos that created rational creatures, indeed all creatures, in accordance with the pre-existent *logoi* of their natures, the principles by which they were created and by which they, through voluntary movement, "ascend to the Logos by whom [they were] created and in whom all things will ultimately be restored."[33]

If Maximus's discussion of the Logos and *logoi* that has just been outlined is indeed the christological specification of his earlier account of creation's movement toward God and of rational creatures' being, well-being, and eternal well-being, then it shows how Maximus's discussion of virtue is a microcosm of that same account of creation with its Christological specification. Let us consider again the three principles—participation, voluntary movement that is divinely given, and deification—to see how they are at work in this discussion of the Logos and *logoi*. Things participate in God, as we have just seen, when they come into being and continue to be. This was clear from his original discussion of creation; now it has received christological specification insofar as he shows that both coming into being and continuing to be are through the divine Logos in accordance with the *logoi* pre-existent in him. The *logoi* are not merely the pre-existent archetypes of created things; they are also the principles of the natures of the created things by which those things rightly move toward God. The beginning of this movement—being—is called participation in God because rational creatures, as do all other creatures, partake of the *logoi* of their existence in the Logos. Furthermore, because these *logoi* are the principles of movement toward the beginning and final end, for rational creatures they are the principles of voluntary movement by which we move toward God rather than away. They are the principles of our "constant straining" toward God, of that "appropriate movement" by which we move toward God as our final end. Thus he writes, "Each person is a 'portion of God' by the *logos* of virtue in him."[34] This movement is voluntary insofar as it is the free movement of the will; it is given by God insofar as this free movement is implanted in us according to nature in

32. Ibid.
33. Ibid.
34. Ibid., 1084D.

the *logoi*. Thus the life of virtue, voluntary movement toward God in accordance with God-given nature, is a life in accordance with, a life that rightly expresses, the principle of our *logoi* in accordance with which we were created by the Logos. Furthermore, the way of this appropriate movement and its end is our experiencing deification, so that we can appropriately be called "portions of God" both by virtue of our pre-existent *logoi* and by virtue of our deification in and by God.

This final end in God, this rest, Maximus makes clear, is an eternal, impassible sabbath, achieved when one has "turned away from worldly things and returned to his own spiritual resting place."[35] That very turning, which is our participation in God, our voluntary and divinely given activity, and our deification, is nothing other that the life of virtue of that Christ is the substance in each person.

Maximus's cosmic teleology is a christological teleology. But how is this a *Chalcedonian* Christology that is nothing other than his christological account of virtue? The answer for Maximus is this: the union of divine and human in Christ, a union without confusion that does not compromise the unique nature of the human creature, is paradigmatic for the union with God toward which we move in the life of virtue. The three principles regarding Maximus's account of virtues, the same three recapitulated in his account of the creation's cosmic teleology and in its christological specification, are all three thoroughly Chalcedonian in their structure. The participation of the *logoi* in the Logos, and hence Maximus's christological account of our participation in God according to our beginning and being, is Chalcedonian in its structure. The *logoi* inhere in the Logos so that the one Logos is many *logoi*; but the Logos is not identical with the *logoi* nor the *logoi* with the Logos. The Logos remains "himself without confusion, the essential and individually distinctive God, the Logos of God the Father."[36] Secondly, that human voluntary action is also the activity of God comes from Maximus's orthodox view of the two wills in Christ, perfectly aligned yet without compromising the integrity of either. Maximus is talking about the surrendering of the human will so that "through the abundant grace of the Spirit it will be shown that God alone is at work, and in all things there will be only one activity, that of God and

35. Ibid.
36. Ibid., 1077C.

of those worthy of kinship with God."[37] While later Maximus will stop speaking of one activity, for fear of its monenergist implications, he here clearly maintains the integrity of the human and divine wills in a way that allows him to speak appropriately, if not literally, of one activity. Finally, it should go without saying that the final deification, our intimate union with God, is patterned after the incarnation in which there is one person, a divinized human, with no confusion of natures. In his conclusion of his discussion of virtue Maximus shows how thoroughly Chalcedonian is his whole discussion of the cosmic teleology of rational beings—indeed of all creation.

> By his gracious condescension God became man and is called man for the sake of man and by exchanging his condition for ours revealed the power that elevates man to God through his love for God and brings God down to man because of his love for man. By this blessed inversion, man is made God by divinization and God is made man by hominization. For the Word of God and God wills always and in all things to accomplish the mystery of his embodiment.[38]

Through the human life of virtue God achieves this embodiment.[39]

ECCLESIAL PARTICIPATION IN THE *MYSTAGOGIA*

If in the discussion of virtue so far it has not been clear why Mamixus is central to an account of ecclesiology and participation, I will show that when this account of virtue, with its Chalcedonian specification and its attention to issues of participation, voluntary activity, and deification, is read in conjunction with Maximus's *Mystagogia* we find that we have the theological moves appropriate to help us to say that through the practices of the church God achieves this embodiment.[40] And just as the previous section was a close reading of *Ambiguum 7*, this section will be a close reading of the *Mystagogia*, with special attention to chapter 1 in which Maximus argues that the church is a figure of God. We will also see how in

37. Ibid.

38. Ibid., 1084C–D.

39. For an account of virtue more broadly in Maximus, see Thurnberg, *Microcosm and Mediator*, 284–330.

40. Maximus, *Church's Mystagogy*, 183–225.

the *Mystagogia* the church's participation in God is visible in the church's visible, virtuous life.

The *Mystagogia* is Maximus's written commentary on the church and its liturgy with a point by point explication of the symbolism of every action of the eucharistic liturgy, from the entrance of the Bishop to the final hymn. Taken together the actions of the liturgy symbolize sacramentally the life of Christ and the eschatological consummation of creation. They enact in the movements of the liturgy the activity of God from the sending of the Son to his bringing creation to its *telos* in God. These activities climax, of course, in the "distribution of the sacrament, which transforms into itself and renders similar to the causal good by grace and participation those who worthily share in it. To them is there lacking nothing of this good that is possible and attainable for men, so that they also can be and be called gods by adoption through grace because God entirely fills them and leaves no part of them empty of his presence."[41] After the above explication of virtue in the context of the Originest controversy, is should be clear in what sense Maximus does and does not understand that participants in the Eucharist can be "called gods by adoption through grace." This does not suggest the negation of the creature/Creator distinction, but rather the divinization of the creature in a way appropriate to the nature of the creature. Three things need to be noticed about this brief reference to divinization. First, divinization is associated with participation in Eucharistic practice; this extends the account of virtue as participation insofar as it suggests the movement from being to well-being, the movement to the human *telos* in the life of God, is accomplished through the movements of the Divine Liturgy. Second, divinization is here referred to in a thoroughly christological context, which is no surprise, in that the Eucharist is a christological practice. Finally, the phrase "adoption by grace" is an allusion to the work of the Holy Spirit, for Maximus has just said with regard to the Lord's Prayer that

> most holy and venerable invocation of our great and blessed God and Father is a symbol of the personal and real adoption to be bestowed through the gift of grace of the Holy Spirit. In accordance with it, once every human particularity is overcome and disclosed by the coming of grace, all the saints will be called sons of God to the extent that from that moment they will have radiantly and

41. Maximus, *Mystagogy*, 203.

gloriously brightened themselves through the virtues with the divine beauty of goodness.[42]

Given the previous exposition of *Ambiguum 7*, it is not inappropriate to read in this reference to virtue an allusion to participation in God through deification. If that is the case, then in a thoroughly christological context (the reception of the Eucharist) and in a Patrological context (the recitation of the "Our Father") Maximus pauses to invoke the particular activity of the Spirit in the journey of participation in God through divinization. It suggests that the practice of the Liturgy, which culminates in the eucharistic practice of participation, is effected through the particular activity of the Spirit's adopting in grace. Thus in two brief paragraphs Maximus has made important theological moves. He has situated divinization in the context of an ecclesial practice, a thoroughly christological practice. In that brief reference to divinization we find contained the whole of his theological system as outlined in the previous section. Most importantly he has articulated the lineaments of a trinitarian account of participation as an ecclesial practice; in the invocation of the *Father* and in the Eucharistic reception of the *Son* Maximus locates the constitutive role in divinization of the *Spirit* in the *activity of the church*. The Spirit's adoption through grace is not an abstract actualization but is a particular and constitutive divine role in the church's participation in God through the liturgical activities. What is often called Maximus's christocentric approach has, it is clear from his explication of the liturgy, a pneumatic center—it is a christocentric-pneumatocentrism.

We must now return to the first chapter of the *Mystagogia*. Here Maximus shows how the "holy Church bears the imprint and image of God since it has the same activity as he does by imitation and in figure."[43] What is this activity of God which the church shares in imitation and figure? It should be familiar from our reading of *Ambiguum 7*. The activity of God is the activity of bringing to union and completion in himself the various and distinct elements of the cosmos, all that possess being. He does this in such a way as not to confuse or deny the distinction, but to establish a unity among the cosmos nonetheless, a unity that reveals through the parts the whole of God's work. I quote Maximus own descrip-

42. Ibid.
43. Ibid., 186.

tion of the activity of God at length, for it is this very activity which the church imitates, the activity of God's bringing the *logoi* to rest in him:

> For God who made and brought into existence all things by his infinite power contains, gathers, and limits them and in his Providence binds both intelligible and sensible beings to himself and to one another. Maintaining about himself as cause, beginning, and end all beings which are by nature distant from one another, he makes them converge in each other by the singular force of their relationship to him as origin. Through this force he leads all beings to a common and unconfused identity of movement and existence, no one being originally in revolt against any other or separated from him by a difference of nature or of movement, but all things combine with all others in an unconfused way by the sin- gular indissoluble relation to and protection of the one principle cause. This reality abolishes and dims all their particular relations considered according to each one's nature, but not by dissolving or destroying them or putting an end to their existence. Rather it does so by transcending them and revealing them, as the whole reveals its parts or as the whole is revealed in its cause by which the same whole and its parts came into being and appearance since they have their whole cause surpassing them in splendor.[44]

This is an account of God as the creation and beginning of all that is and as the agent of its teleological consummation in the unity and diversity that maintains the integrity of the particularity of all that is while at the same time achieving a unity of the cosmos through the united relation- ship of these particularities to their origin. About this activity Maximus writes: "It is in this way that the holy Church of God will be shown to be working for us the same effect as God, in the same way as the image reflects its archetype."[45] The church shares the activity of God precisely because through the church a vast number of people, "who are distinct

---

44. Ibid., 186. Hans Urs von Balthasar says of this first chapter, "These texts are enough to give us a notion of the way the christological formula [of Chalcedon] expands, for Maximus, into a fundamental law of metaphysics. Illuminated by the highest level of theological synthesis—the union of God and the world in Christ—Maximus searches out traces of the development of principles, of the conditions of possibility of this synthesis, and in the process discovers the formal structure of all created being, even the formal structure of the relationship between the absolute and contingent" (von Balthasar, *Cosmic Liturgy*, 70). This is precisely what I tried to argue in relationship to virtue in *Ambiguum* 7, that the union of God and the world is given in terms of Chalcedonian Christology.

45. Maximus, *Mystagogy*, 187.

from one another and vastly different by birth and appearance, by nationality and language, by customs and age, by opinions and skills, by manners and habits, by pursuits and studies," are reborn and recreated through the Spirit. "To all," Maximus writes, "and in equal measure it [the church] gives and bestows one divine form and designation, to be Christ's and to carry his name."[46] It is through the activity of the church that the one body of Christ exists and appears as it is formed of different members. For "It is [Christ] who encloses in himself all beings by the unique, simple, and infinitely wise power of his goodness." Maximus is making this crucial point: The church *images* the activity of God by *performing* the activity of God of reconciling into one body—Christ's—people from all ages, nations, races, and stations. To be a reflection and an archetype is, in this case, deeper than how "image" is usually taken. In this case the image participates in what it images insofar as it shares that one's activity. The church's practice, we can say on the basis of Maximus, is not different from the practice of God; furthermore, the church practices this reconciliation as the body of Christ: "Thus to *be* and to *appear* as one body formed of different members is really worthy of Christ himself." We saw in the discussion of virtue in Maximus how it is not a contradiction to say that God and a human share the same activity because of the noncompetitive relationship between divine and human wills. Here the same point is extended to the church with its implicit Chalcedonian justification. As the church *is* Christ's body, and thus, as it *appears* as Christ's body—for to "be" in the case of the church is to "be visible"—the church images the activity of God by *performing* the activity of God, thus making the activity of God itself visible in the world. Or, to adopt the phrase from the end of the previous section, through the activity of the church God achieves embodiment. Maximus concludes the first chapter thus:

> Thus, it has been said, the holy Church of God is an image of God because it realizes the same union of the faithful with God. As different as they are by language, places, and customs, they are made one by [the church] through faith. God realizes this union among the nature of things without confusing them but in lessening and bringing together their distinction, as was shown, in a relationship and union with himself as cause, principle, and end.[47]

46. Ibid.
47. Ibid., 187–88.

The church is an *image* of God because it *realizes* our union with God. But it can also be inferred: the church realizes *itself* in this union with God precisely because the church is what is being realized here, the reconciliation of all things into one body. To use my language: The church practices itself as it practices the activity of God; and since this activity is the reconciliation of all things in Christ, it is Christ himself through his body, the church, who practices himself, performing his identity as the center of all that is. And this is done, in Chalcedonian fashion, without the confusion or destruction of the createdness of the church itself. It is precisely as the body of united humans that the church is Christ's body practicing itself. Andrew Louth summarizes nicely Maximus's ecclesiology: "[That the church is a hierarchy] does mean order but, like the structure of the church building as Maximos explains it, it is an order drawing and being drawn up to union with God, and more than that it is a matter of knowledge and activity. It is in this sense that the church, for Maximus is hierarchical; there is order and structure, manifest not least in the ranks of the ministers, that enables the church as a community to be ordered towards God, to be an instrument of God's outreach towards those who do not know him or who misunderstand him, to be a place where God's activity is encountered and knowledge of God shared."[48] The church is the embodied and ordered participation in the activity and life of God.

I have been arguing throughout that the church's participation in God is marked by a peculiar visibility; it has a particular shape, which is the shape of Christ's peaceable existence in the world. At the end of the *Mystagogia* Maximus turns his attention to the shape of the faithful life. As we would expect from his account of participation and virtue, participation in the divine life for Maximus does have the shape of faithfulness in the world. In chapter 24 of the *Mystagogia* Maximus summarizes his account of the distinct but united church community and that community's participation in the activity of God through the practice of the liturgy. The summary extends the original analysis in that it makes explicit reference to the shape of the deification received through participation in the liturgy. Having reminded the reader of the grace of the Spirit that comes through the praying of the Lord's prayer and the participation in the Eucharist, Maximus remarks,

---

48. Louth, "Ecclesiology of Saint Maximos the Confessor," 113.

The clear proof of this grace is the voluntary disposition of good will toward those akin to us whereby the man who needs our help in any way becomes as much as possible our friend as God is and we do not leave him abandoned and forsaken but rather with fitting zeal we show him in action the disposition which is alive in us with respect to God and our neighbor. For a work is proof of a disposition. . . . For if the Word has shown that the one who is in need of having good done to him is God—for as long, he tells us, as you did it for one of these least one, you did it for me—on God's very word, then, he will much more show that the one who can do good and who does it is truly God by grace and participation because he has taken on in happy imitation the energy and characteristic of [God's] own doing good. And if the poor man is God, it is because of God's condescension in becoming poor for us and in taking upon himself by his own suffering the sufferings of each one and "until the end of time," always suffering mystically out of goodness in proportion to each one's suffering.[49]

It has been argued that Christologies that emphasize the "cosmic Christ," as Maximus is well known to do, distract from the importance of a life of following Jesus, a life of discipleship.[50] Furthermore, as I have already shown, certain accounts of participation similarly abstract from the materially embodied nature of ecclesial activity and Christian discipleship. But what Maximus has taught us—what Chalcedon taught us before—was that there is no following Jesus without the cosmic Christ and there is no cosmic Christ without a Jesus to follow. This is nowhere clearer than

49. Maximus, *Mystagogy*, 211–12.

50. John Howard Yoder has argued that appeals in some way to cosmic Christology in contemporary ethics is a strategy to find a normative ethics beyond the particularity of Jesus that can speak to the wider world. He writes, "The temptation soon arises to be freed from the limits of Jesus' earthliness, Jewishness, and cross. We often speak of this temptation as 'gnostic,' because one of its early forms sought to describe a 'larger Christ than Jesus' by incorporating into a speculative system the contribution of other paths to wisdom. But there are analogies to Gnosticism as well in the advocacy of 'larger' views of the historical process. Some appeal to the Father, others to the Spirit, others to the 'Cosmic Christ' or to the Trinity as a whole as warrants for learning from 'creation' or 'nature' or 'history' other lessons than those of the incarnation. Have we other standards than those of the crucified rabbi to recognize what we shall accredit as 'liberation' or as 'humane'?" (Yoder, *For The Nations*, 242). Yoder rightly critiques how purported cosmic Christologies are used to justify actions beyond those shown to be faithful by the life of Jesus. Maximus, on the other hand, uses the Cosmic Christ to show how the church should be formed in the very image of the one who, in his earthy Jewishness and in no other way, lived the life of God.

in this passage. Maximus here shows that participation in the activity of God through the body of Christ—that is, Christ's practicing himself in the Spirit as the church—is proven and visible in the witness of those who follow the commands of Jesus, but not only the commands. Participation and imitation are here synonymous; as our participation in the life of God becomes visible it acquires the peculiar shape of the life of Jesus, who is the condescension of God. The shape of "God's own doing good" is the shape of Jesus's willful and non-violent suffering on behalf of others. If that is the shape of God's own doing good it will be the shape of the church and the Christian life that truly participates in the active life of God.

CONCLUSION

Part Three began in chapter 5 by looking at accounts of participation in three authors. Through the discussion of the work of those theologians I began to outline what might be called criteria for an account of participation: 1) An account of participation must faithfully maintain the distinction between Creator and creature. 2) An account of participation must be given in terms of the particular and embodied nature of the church. 3) An account of participation must begin with the particularity of Christ and the church and not in a general account of creation's participation in God *qua* creation. Creation's participation can only be understood teleologically, as a movement toward an ever deepening participation in God through what Jenson calls the gateway of the church. 4) An account of participation will show how participation in God is not an invisible essence or interiority, but is socially visible and has the shape of the life of Jesus' peacableness. And 5), any faithful account of the church's participation in God must be given full trinitarian specification.

In this chapter I turned to Maximus the Confessor. His thoroughgoing Chalcedonian Christology coupled with his apophatic theology allows him to articulate an account of participation that shows how the above five criteria are indeed possible and appropriate for any account of participation. Most importantly, Maximus in an important way argues that participation in God's life is visible just to the extent that the shape is of Jesus's own participation in God's life. And that shape was the shape of a suffering servant. When the world sees Christ's availability to the world in the body called the church, when the world sees Christ practicing himself in the Spirit, the world will see the people of God embodied in its corporate life the peculiar visibility of servanthood, suffering, and peaceableness. This particular visibility, as Maximus, and Bonhoeffer and McCabe, have shown is in no way *opposed* to a Christology of participation, or to a cosmic Christology, but is rather a constitutive element of any adequate account of participation that takes its beginning from the embodied participation that is the man Jesus.

Conclusion

IN THE INTRODUCTION, A look at the practices of early Methodist so-cieties and classes and at the worshiping life of Mt. Level Missionary Baptist Church raised three guiding questions for an understanding of church practices as the church's participation in God:

- How should the relationship between the embodied, human practices of ecclesial communities and the activity of God be understood?

- How can church practices and their participation in God be ar-ticulated in a way that takes with utter seriousness the clearly embodied nature of these practices?

- How do the practices of these communities orient the rest of cre-ation to God's life as well?

In this book I have been arguing that these questions are best an-swered with a theology of church practices that says: *the church's partici-pation in God is none other than Christ's practicing himself as the embodied practices of the church, in the Spirit, on behalf of the world. Moreover, this practicing, this participation, has a peculiar visibility, because it is the Jesus of the Gospels who practices himself in the church; this visibility of the form of Jesus shows the world the shape of its own* telos *in God.* Along the way I have said that several things must be true about such an account of par-ticipation in order for it to be appropriate to the lived experience of the church and to the Gospel that the church embodies. Here, I unpack this theology of church practices.

CHURCH AS CHRIST'S PRACTICING HIMSELF

The church is *Christ's practicing himself.* Embedded in this account of the church are several theological claims. First, we have here an identification between Christ and the church. The only way it makes sense to see the church as participating in God is to see how the church is taken up into the incarnation. So, as Bonhoeffer and Jenson both argue, in the church's embodiment Christ's own embodiment is available for the world. The emphasis here is on the *is*. The church does not merely *reflect* Christ in the world, as if Christ is somewhere else, but the church *is* Christ and thus is a participation in God's "roominess."

Second, to say the church is Christ's practicing himself is to show that the activity of the church is constituted by both divine and human activity, and is thus in the broadest sense sacramental. This claim entails the rejection of a general principle of sacramentality of all creation in favor of a particular understanding of the sacramentality of the church's activity because of the particular constitution of the church in its divine and human agency. I think John Howard Yoder makes most clear this kind of particular sacramentality when he notes that in the bodily practices of the church, "Each of [the five practices Yoder discusses], first of all, is a wholly human, empirically accessible practice—nothing esoteric. Yet each is, according to the apostolic writers, an act of God. God does not merely authorize or command them. *God* is *doing* them in, with, and under the human practice."[1] When one understands the church in terms of Chalcedonian orthodoxy, one can say quite explicitly that the church's activity is both divine and human, without contradiction, and in a way that is not true for all of creation's participation in God. This Chalcedonian principle was made most explicit in the discussion of virtue in Maximus the Confessor. There we saw how virtue is both voluntary activity and God's activity. Applied to the church, Maximus shows us how, as Christ's continued presence in the world, the church participates in God in a way that does not negate the full humanness of the church.

Furthermore, to say the church is Christ's practicing himself is to emphasize the corporate, embodied sociality of the church. The church is Christ's presence in the world, and thus its visible participation in God, not on the basis of some supposed transcendent interiority, but precisely in its corporately embodied human activity, the internal goods of which are the activities themselves as they are participation in God. Here the full weight of McCabe's Wittgensteinian-Thomism comes to bear. The word *practicing* in this account is meant to carry precisely this understanding of human embodiment and so militate against any false dichotomies,

1. Yoder, *Royal Priesthood*, 369.

essentialist interiorities, or idealist invisibilities so prevalent in discussions of the nature of the church. In this sense, then, Christ's practicing himself *for the world* is redundant, because, as we saw in McCabe and Bonhoeffer, Christ's embodiment, precisely because this is *body*, is Christ's "for the world"; it is his availability. Finally, the word *practicing* is meant to convey the important point that participation is a teleological activity. It is not best understood as that quality of creation precisely as it is created, but rather as the church's activity, participation is the activity of a person. There is no inappropriate *stasis* implied in participation.

The church is Christ's practicing himself *in the Spirit*. An account of the church's participation cannot be given in general terms of creation's being, but rather must be given in the full particularity of the God of Christian worship, a God who is Father, Son, and Holy Spirit, since participation is participation in this God's activity of being God. The phrase *in the Spirit* here does two things. First, it names the distinction between Christ and the church—claimed by both Bonhoeffer and Jenson, but given no real specificity—entailed in the very identification of the two. Here we must be reminded of Cyril of Alexandria's pneumatology. Cyril could not discuss the particular mission of the Spirit in the church abstracted from an understanding of the work of the Spirit in the incarnation, a work clearly displayed at several places in the Scripture. It could be said that the Spirit plays a central role in the enhypostatic/anhypostatic union. But, as we saw in Maximus's pneumatology, the role of the Spirit with regard to the church is different, precisely because it has the role of "adopting." The church is adopted into the union of the divine and human in Jesus in a way that is distinct from the incarnation precisely because the enhypostatic/anhypostatic union says that there was no man Jesus to be adopted apart from his hypostasis in the divine *Logos*. But there is a humanity—both Jewish and Gentile—prior to the church that is adopted by the Spirit, thus made participant by grace in the incarnation, though it is theologically incoherent on the basis of Chalcedon to say that the man Jesus was made a partaker by grace in the incarnation. So it can be said: The difference between Christ and the church is that the Spirit makes the church Christ in a way that, on the basis of Chalcedon, it is impossible to say that the Spirit makes the man Jesus the incarnate Son.

Second, the phrase *in the Spirit* once again distinguishes between the practices of the church and the practices of other communities. *In the Spirit* means that the activity of the Spirit's adopting the church, making it "apt," as Robert Jenson says, to be united to the Son[2]—the activity of the Spirit that allows for a distinction between Christ and the church within the very identification of Christ and the church—is the same activity that distinguishes between the divine activity that constitutes the church and the divine activity that constitutes other social bodies. However we speak about God's activity in other human social bodies or in the rest of creation, we certainly don't speak of it in this way.

That the church is Christ's practicing himself in the Spirit *on behalf of the world* is, as I suggested, redundant when one understands, following Bonhoeffer, McCabe, and Jenson, that the embodied activity of the church, insofar as the church is Christ's body, is Christ's availability to the world. The shape of the church's participation is always, by its very nature, for the world, just as Christ, Bonhoeffer tells us, is always *pro nobis*.

THE SHAPE OF PARTICIPATION

The church's participation in God has a shape. It has a peculiar visibility which is the form of Jesus. When the early Methodists heard the field preachers urge them that "Now is the day of salvation," when they joined the societies, when they joined a class and confessed their sins and engaged in works of piety and mercy, when they went to their local Anglican church whenever the Eucharist was being celebrated, these early Methodist communities were displaying their participation in the life of God. They were not manifesting outwardly an inward essence. Nor were they joining God's already constituted activity somewhere else. They were "spreading Scriptural holiness across the land," because their own visibility was the visibility of Christ, and thus the activity of God—Christ as he continued to practice his suffering servanthood on behalf of the world. As Albert Outler has nicely put it, writing about evangelism in early Methodism, "The Word made *audible* must become the Word made *visible*, if men's lives are ever to be touched by the 'Word made flesh.' . . . [F]or Wesley understood as we seem to have forgotten, that it is the Word *made visible*

---

2. "Orthodoxy exhorts the West to recognize in this event [Pentecost] a specific church-instituting act of the Spirit, which emerges just from his identity as Spirit. We may summarily describe it: the Spirit *frees* an actual human community from merely historical determinisms, to be apt to be united with the Son and thus to be the gateway of creation's translation into God" (Jenson, *Works of God*, 179). The enhypostatic/anhypostatic union forbids us from saying that the Spirit makes the man Jesus free from historical determinisms and apt to be united to the Logos, as I argued above.

in the lives of practicing, witnessing lay Christians that constitutes the church's most powerful evangelistic witness."[3] For John Wesley, 2 Peter 1:4 was of central significance for understanding this visibility: holiness, the material sanctification of believers joined together in one body—their being renewed in the image of God—was none other than their partaking of the divine nature.

Dietrich Bonhoeffer's understanding that in preaching "church preaches to church" is clearly displayed when the Christians of Mt. Level Missionary Baptist Church in Durham, NC gather for worship on Sunday morning. While the service of worship climaxes in the preacher's sermon, only a few minutes in their midst makes palpably clear that their entire communal existence is an embodied proclamation. From the lay-led pastoral prayer to the choral anthem to the embodied witness of the believers hearing the sermon being proclaimed, this activity puts into question any notion of preaching as "an independent trade," as the special provenance of the clergyperson in his or her study. The whole service of worship, even the pastor's praying the eucharistic prayers, is an embodiment of the gospel's proclamation.

But this corporate, embodied proclamation is also the visibility of the Spirit's work in the lives of these witnesses. Here, in a proclamation that extends into their ministries and lives throughout the week, they are irradiated with the Spirit so they shine into the world like a stained glass window. They are the icon of the Savior in the world, the visible, tangible presence of Christ for their neighbors, for through the Spirit, "God nurtures us, guides us, forms us into the image of Christ, making us partakers of the divine nature."[4] In both of these communities, the body of Christ is visible to the world. But that visibility has a significant corollary. Through their witness, through the witness of their corporate practices, the rest of the world sees its true end and destiny. It sees in this very shape, in the shape of the suffering, peaceable servanthood of Christ as it is being practiced in the Spirit, its true calling and destiny, the very shape toward which it is moving as created and redeemed by God. Again Yoder:

> For a practice to qualify as "evangelical" in the functional sense means first of all that it communicates *news*. It says something particular that would not be known and could not be believed were

3. Outler, *Evangelism and Theology*, 22.
4. W. Turner, *Discipleship*, 11.

it not said. Second, it must mean functionally that this "news" is attested as *good*; as *shalom*. . . . It tells the world what is the world's own calling and destiny, not by announcing either a utopian or a realistic goal to be imposed on the whole society, but by pioneering a paradigmatic demonstration of both the power and the practices that define the shape of restored humanity. The confessing people of God is the new world on its way.[5]

Or, as we have already seen Herbert McCabe say, the church exists "to show the world to itself"—that is, to show the world its future in God.[6] The church now, in its corporate life, shows the world its own future as that toward and through which it is being drawn into God's own life. Robert Jenson, in a phrase reminiscent of Maximus the Confessor's cosmic teleology, is surely right when he says, "All God's creatures are moved by God it their fulfillment in him; the church is doubly so moved, as one among God's creatures and as the creature that embodies that movement for others."[7]

It is not hubristic to make this kind of claim about real and fallible communities like the societies of early Methodism or a Baptist Church in North Carolina. It is part of the mystery of Christ's incarnation that in his humility, servanthood, and peaceableness, participation should be made visible; it is part of the grace of sharing in that mystery that the church claims through its own practiced servanthood that God's life is made visible as the *telos* of all creation.

In the end, the argument of this book can be viewed as an extended commentary on the ecclesial reality of 2 Peter 1:4. But these words cannot show participation in God; they cannot show the world to itself. The finest commentary on 2 Peter 1:4 is the lived practices of real church communities living, in all their earthiness, the life of God in the world.

5. Yoder, *Royal Priesthood*, 373.
6. McCabe, *Law*, 147.
7. Jenson, *Works of God*, 172.

Bibliography

Albin, Thomas, R. "An Empirical Study of Early Methodist Spirituality." In *Wesleyan Theology Today: A Bicentennial Theological Consultation*, edited by Theodore Runyon, 275–90. Nashville: Kingswood, 1985.

Allchin, A. M. *Participation in God: A Forgotten Strand in Anglican Theology*. Wilton, CT: Morehouse-Barelow, 1988.

Anscombe, G. E. M. *Intention*. 2nd ed. Cambridge: Harvard University Press, 1963.

Avram, Wesley D. "The Work of Conscience in Bonhoeffer's Homiletic." *Homiletic* 19 (2004) 1–14.

Ballard, Bruce W. *Understanding MacIntyre*. New York: University Press of America, 2000.

Bass, Diane Butler. *The Practicing Congregation: Imagining a New Old Church*. Herndon, VA: Alban Institute, 2004.

Bass, Dorothy C., editor. *Practicing Our Faith: A Way of Life for a Searching People*. San Francisco: Jossey-Bass, 1997.

Bethge, Eberhard. *Dietrich Bonhoeffer: A Biography*. Rev. ed. Translated by Eric Mosbacher. Minneapolis: Fortress, 2000.

Bonhoeffer, Dietrich. *Christ the Center*. Translated by Edwin H. Robertson. New York: Harper Collins, 1978.

———. *Discipleship*. Translated by Barbara Green and Reinhard Krauss. Dietrich Bonhoeffer Works English 4. Minneapolis: Fortress, 2001.

———. *Life Together/Prayerbook of the Bible*. Translated by Daniel W. Bloesch and Names H. Burtness. Dietrich Bonhoeffer Works English 5. Minneapolis: Fortress, 1996.

———. *Meditations on the Word*. 2nd ed. Translated by David McI. Gracie. Cambridge: Cowley, 2000.

———. *Sanctorum Communio*. Translated by Reinhard Krauss and Nancy Lukens. Dietrich Bonhoeffer Works English 1. Minneapolis: Fortress, 1998.

———. *A Testament to Freedom*. Edited by Geffrey B. Kelly and F. Burton Nelson. New York: Harper Collins, 2000.

———. *Worldly Preaching: Lectures on Homiletics*. Translated and edited by Clyde E. Fant. New York: Crossroad, 1991.

Bowmer, John C. *The Sacrament of the Lord's Supper in Early Methodism*. London: Dacre, 1951.

Buckley, James, and David Yeago, editors. *Knowing the Triune God: The Work of the Spirit in the Practices of the Church*. Grand Rapids: Eerdmans, 2001.

Burrell, David B. *Knowing the Unkowable God: Ibn-Sina, Maimonides, Aquinas*. Notre Dame, IN: University of Notre Dame Press, 1986.

Carter, Craig. *The Politics of the Cross: The Theology and Social Ethics of John Howard Yoder*. Grand Rapids: Brazos, 2001.

Bibliography

Campbell, Charles L. *Preaching Jesus: New Directions for Homiletics in Hans Frei's Postliberal Theology*. Grand Rapids: Eerdmans, 1997.

Cavanaugh, William. *Theopolitical Imagination: Discovering the Liturgy as a Political Act in an Age of Global Consumerism*. London: T. & T. Clark, 2002.

———. *Torture and Eucharist*. Challenges in Contemporary Theology Series. Oxford: Blackwell, 1998.

Cobb, John Jr., and David Ray Griffin. *Process Theology: An Introductory Exposition*. Philadelphia: Westminster, 1976.

Cyril of Alexandria. *Commentary on John XI, II*. In *Documents in Early Christian Thought*, edited and translated by Maurice Wiles and Mark Santer, 168–71. Cambridge: Cambridge University Press, 1975.

de Gruchy, John W., editor. *The Cambridge Companion to Dietrich Bonhoeffer*. Cambridge: Cambridge University Press, 1999.

de Lange, Frits. *Waiting for the Word: Dietrich Bonhoeffer on Speaking about God*. Translated by Marin N. Walton. Grand Rapids: Eerdmans, 1995.

de Lubac, Henri. *The Motherhood of the Church*. Translated by Sr. Sergia Englund, OCD. San Francisco: Ignatius, 1982.

Doyle, Dennis M. *Communion Ecclesiology: Vision and Versions*. Maryknoll, NY: Orbis, 2000.

Dulles, Avery. *Models of the Church*. Expanded ed. New York: Doubleday, 2002.

Dykstra, Craig. "Reconceiving Practice in Theological Inquiry and Education." In *Virtues and Practices in the Christian Tradition: Christian Ethics after MacIntyre*, edited by Nancy Murphy, Brad J. Kallenberg, and Mark Thiessen Nation, 191–82. Harrisburg, PA: Trinity, 1997.

Dykstra, Craig, and Dorothy Bass. "A Theological Understanding of Christian Practices." In *Practicing Theology: Belief and Practices in Christian Life*, edited by Miroslav Volf and Dorothy Bass, 13–32. Grand Rapids: Eerdmans, 2002.

Eagleton, Terry. *The Body as Language: Outline of a "New Left" Theology*. London: Sheed & Ward, 1970.

Edwards, James C. *Ethics without Philosophy: Wittgenstein and the Moral Life*. Tampa: University Presses of Florida, 1985.

Ford, David S. *Self and Salvation: Being Transformed*. Cambridge: Cambridge University Press, 1999.

Fowl, Stephen E., and L. Gregory Jones. *Reading in Communion: Scripture and Ethics in Christian Life*. Grand Rapids: Eerdmans, 1991.

Frazer, Elizabeth, and Nicola Lacey. "MacIntyre, Feminism and the Concept of Practice." In *After MacIntyre: Critical Perspectives on the Work of Alasdair MacIntyre*, edited by John Horton and Susan Mendus, 265–82. Notre Dame, IN: University of Notre Dame Press, 1994.

Frei, Hans W. *The Eclipse of Biblical Narrative: A Study in Eighteenth and Nineteenth Century Hermeneutics*. New Haven: Yale University Press, 1974.

Green, Clifford J. *Bonhoeffer: A Theology of Sociality*. Rev. ed. Grand Rapids: Eerdmans, 1999.

Griffiths, Paul J. *Lying: An Augustinian Theology of Duplicity*. Grand Rapids: Brazos, 2004.

Gustafson, James M. *Treasure in Earthen Vessels: The Church as a Human Community*. New York: Harper & Row, 1961.

Hauerwas, Stanley. *Performing the Faith: Bonhoeffer and the Practice of Nonviolence*. Grand Rapids: Brazos, 2004.

Bibliography

Hauerwas, Stanley, and Charles Pinches. *Christians Among the Virtues: Theological Conversations on Modern Ethics*. Notre Dame, IN: University of Notre Dame Press, 1997.

Healy, Nicholas. *Church, World and the Christian Life*. Cambridge Studies in Christian Doctrine. Cambridge: Cambridge Uni-versity Press, 2000.

Heitzenrater, Richard P. *Wesley and the People Called Methodists*. Nashville: Abingdon, 1995.

Hick, John, editor. *The Myth of God Incarnate*. London: SCM, 1977.

Hütter, Reinhard. *Suffering Divine Things: Theology as Church Practice*. Translated by Doug Scott. Grand Rapids: Eerdmans, 2000.

Hughes, Graham. *Worship as Meaning: A Liturgical Theology for Later Modernity*. Cambridge: Cambridge University Press, 2000.

Jenson, Robert W. "The Church and the Sacraments." In *The Cambridge Companion to Christian Doctrine*, edited by Colin E. Gunton and Daniel Hardy, 207–25. Cambridge: Cambridge University Press, 2003.

———. *The Triune God*. Vol. 1 of *Systematic Theology*. New York: Oxford University Press, 1997.

———. *The Works of God*. Vol. 2 of *Systematic Theology*. New York: Oxford University Press, 1999.

Jones, L. Gregory, and Kevin R. Armstrong. *Resurrecting Excellence: Shaping Faithful Christian Ministry*, edited by Jackson W. Carroll. Grand Rapids: Eerdmans, 2006.

Kallenberg, Brad J. "The Master Argument of MacIntyre's *After Virtue*." In *Virtues and Practices in the Christian Tradition*, edited by Nancy Murphy, Brad J. Kallenberg, and Mark Thiessen Nation, 7–29. Harrisburg, PA: Trinity, 1997.

Keating, Daniel A. *The Appropriation of the Divine Life in Cyril of Alexandria*. Oxford: Oxford University Press, 2004.

Kenneson, Philip D. *Beyond Sectarianism: Re-imagining Church and World*. Harrisburg, PA: Trinity, 1999.

———. "The Reappearance of the Visible Church: An Analysis of Production and Reproduction of Christian Identity." PhD diss., Duke University, 1991.

Kerr, Fergus. *Theology after Wittgenstein*. London: SPCK, 1997.

Lash, Nicholas. *Theology on the Way to Emmaus*. London: SCM, 1986.

Lindbeck, George. *The Nature of Doctrine: Religion and Theology in a Postliberal Age*. Philadelphia: Westminster, 1984.

Lischer, Richard. *The End of Words: The Language of Reconciliation in a Culture of Violence*. Grand Rapids: Eerdmans, 2005.

Long, D. Stephen. *John Wesley's Moral Theology: The Quest for God and Goodness*. Nashville: Kingswood, 2005.

Lossky, Vladimir. *The Mystical Theology of the Eastern Church*. Crestwood, NY: St. Vladimir's Seminary Press, 1976.

Louth, Andrew. "The Ecclesiology of Saint Maximos the Confessor." *International Journal for the Study of the Christian Church* 4 (2004) 109–20.

———. *Maximus the Confessor*. London: Routledge, 1996.

Lowry, Eugene. *The Homiletical Plot: The Sermon as Narrative Art Form*. Atlanta: Knox, 1978.

———. *The Sermon: Dancing at the Edge of Mystery*. Nashville: Abingdon, 1997.

Lumen Gentium. In *The Sixteen Documents of Vatican II*, edited by Marianne Lorraine Trouve, 123–99. Boston: Pauline, 1999.

Bibliography

Maddox, Randy L. *Responsible Grace: John Wesley's Practical Theology.* Nashville: Kingswood, 1994.

———. "Recent Research on St. Maximus the Confessor: A Survey." *St. Vladimir's Theological Quarterly* 42 (1998) 67–84.

Maximus Confessor. *On the Cosmic Mystery of Jesus Christ: Selected Writings from St. Maximus the Confessor.* Translated by Paul M. Blowers and Robert Louis Wilkin. Crestwood, NY: St. Vladimir's Seminary Press, 2003.

———. *Maximus Confessor: Selected Writings.* Translated by George C. Berthold. New York: Paulist, 1985.

Marsh, Charles. *Reclaiming Dietrich Bonhoeffer: The Promise of His Theology.* New York: Oxford University Press, 1994.

MacIntyre, Alasdair. *After Virtue.* 2nd ed. Notre Dame, IN: University of Notre Dame Press, 1984.

———. *Dependant Rational Animals: Why Human Beings Need the Virtues.* Chicago: Open Court, 1999.

———. *Three Rival Versions of Moral Enquiry: Encyclopaedia, Genealogy, and Tradition.* Notre Dame, IN: University of Notre Dame Press, 1990.

———. *Whose Justice? Which Rationality?* Notre Dame, IN: University of Notre Dame Press, 1988.

McCabe, Herbert. *God, Christ and Us.* Edited by Brian Davies, OP. London: Continuum, 2003.

———. *God Matters.* Springfield, IL: Templegate, 1987.

———. *God Still Matters.* Edited by Brian Davies, OP. London: Continuum, 2002.

———. *Law, Love, and Language.* 1968. Reprint, New York: Continuum, 2003.

———. *The People of God: The Fullness of Life in the Church.* New York: Sheed & Ward, 1964.

———. *The Teaching of the Catholic Church: A New Catechism of Christian Doctrine.* Maryknoll, NY: Orbis, 1985.

McClendon, James Wm. *Ethics: Systematic Theology,* vol. 1. Nashville: Abingdon, 1986.

McGuckin, John. *Saint Cyril of Alexandria and the Christological Controversy: Its History, Theology, and Texts.* Crestwood, NY: St. Vladimir's Seminary Press, 2004.

McParltan, Paul. *Sacrament of Salvation: An Introduction to Eucharistic Ecclesiology.* Edinburgh: T. & T. Clark, 1995.

Milbank, John. *Being Reconciled: Ontology and Pardon.* London: Routledge, 2003.

———. *Theology and Social Theory: Beyond Secular Reason.* Oxford: Blackwell, 1990.

———. *The Word Made Strange: Theology, Language, Culture.* Oxford: Blackwell, 1997.

Milbank, John, and Catherine Pickstock. *Truth in Aquinas.* London: Routledge, 2001.

Milbank, John, Catherine Pickstock, and Graham Ward, editors. *Radical Orthodoxy.* London: Routledge, 1999.

Newbigin, Leslie. *The Open Secret: An Introduction to the Theology of Mission.* Rev. ed. Grand Rapids: Eerdmans, 1995.

Nichols, Aidan. *Byzantine Gospel: Maximus the Confessor in Modern Scholarship.* Edinburgh: T. & T. Clark, 1993.

———. *Catholic Thought Since the Enlightenment: A Survey.* Pretoria: Unisa, 1998.

———. *Dominican Gallery.* Heredfordshire, UK: Gracewing, 1997.

———. *The Holy Eucharist: From the New Testament to Pope John Paul II.* Dublin: Veritas, 1991.

Niebuhr, H. Richard. *The Meaning of Revelation.* New York: MacMillan, 1946.

Bibliography

Outler, Albert C. *Evangelism and Theology in the Wesleyan Spirit*. Nashville: Discipleship, 1996.

Owens, L. Roger. "Free, Present, and Faithful: A Theological Reading of the Character of God in Exodus." *New Blackfriars* 85 (2004) 614–27.

———. "Jesus Christ Is His Own Rhetoric! Reflections on the Relationship between Theology and Rhetoric in Preaching." *Currents in Theology and Mission* 32 (2005) 187–94.

———. "Sabbath-Keeping: Sabbath-Keeping and the Desire for Justice." In *Vital Christianity: Spirituality, Justice, and Christian Practice*, edited by David L. Weaver-Zercher and William H. Willimon, 2005. New York: T. & T. Clark, 2005.

———. "The Theological Ethics of Herbert McCabe, OP: A Review Essay." *Journal of Religious Ethics* 33 (2005) 571–92.

Rattenbury, J. Ernst. *The Eucharistic Hymns of John and Charles Wesley*. Edited by Timothy J. Crouch. Akron, OH: OSL, 1996.

Reno, R. R. *In the Ruins of the Church: Sustaining Faith in an Age of Diminished Christianity*. Grand Rapids: Brazos, 2002.

Robinson, John A. T. *The Body: A Study in Pauline Theology*. London: SCM, 1952.

Runyon, Theodore. *The New Creation: John Wesley's Theology Today*. Nashville: Abingdon, 1998.

Schindler, David L. *Heart of the World, Center of the Church: Communio Ecclesiology, Liberalism, and Liberation*. Grand Rapid: Eerdmans, 1996.

Schleiermacher, Friedrich. *The Christian Faith*. Translated and edited by H. R. Mackintosh and J. S. Stewart. Edinburgh: T. & T. Clark, 1989.

Schmemann, Alexander. *For the Life of the World*. Crestwood, NY: St. Vladimir's Seminary Press, 1973.

Schoof, Mark. *A Survey of Catholic Theology: 1800–1970*. Translated by N. D. Smith. New York: Paulist Newman Press, 1970.

Smith, James K. A. *Introducing Radical Orthodoxy: Mapping a Post-secular Theology*. Grand Rapids: Baker, 2004.

Sopko, Andrew J. "Bonhoeffer: An Orthodox Ecclesiology?" *Greek Orthodox Review* 28 (1983) 81–88.

Tanner, Kathryn. *Jesus, Humanity and the Trinity: A Brief Systematic Theology*. Minneapolis: Fortress, 2001.

Taylor, Barbara Brown. *Home By Another Way*. Cambridge, MA: Cowley, 1999.

———. *The Preaching Life*. Cambridge, MA: Cowley, 1993.

Thurnberg, Lars. *Microcosm and Mediator: The Theological Anthropology of Maximus the Confessor*. 2nd ed. Chicago: Open Court, 1995.

Torrance, T. F. *Royal Priesthood*. Edinburgh: Oliver & Boyd, 1955.

Turner, Denys. *Faith, Reason, and the Existence of God*. Cambridge: Cambridge University Press, 2004.

———. *Faith Seeking*. London: SCM, 2002.

Turner, William C. *Discipleship for African American Christians: A Journey through the Church Covenant*. Valley Forge, PA: Judson, 2002.

———. "Preaching The Spirit: The Liberation of Preaching." Unpublished collection of sermons preached at Mt. Level Missionary Baptist Church, Durham, NC.

Volf, Miroslav. *After Our Likeness: The Church as the Image of the Trinity*. Sacra Doctrina: Christian Theology for a Postmodern Age. Grand Rapids: Eerdmans, 1998.

Bibliography

Volf, Miroslav, and Dorothy Bass, editors. *Practicing Theology: Beliefs and Practices in Christian Life*. Grand Rapids: Eerdmans, 2002.

von Balthasar, Hans Urs. *Cosmic Liturgy: The Universe According to Maximus the Confessor*. Translated by Brian E. Daley, SJ. San Francisco: Ignatius, 2003.

———. *Explorations in Theology*. Spouse of the Word 2. San Fransisco: Ignatius, 1991.

Wainwright, Geoffrey. *Worship with One Accord: Where Liturgy and Ecumenism Embrace*. New York: Oxford University Press, 1997.

Watson, David Lowes. *The Early Methodist Class Meeting*. Nashville: Discipleship, 1985.

Weaver-Zercher, David, and William Willimon, editors. *Vital Christianity: Spirituality, Justice, and Christian Practice*. New York: T. & T. Clark, 2005.

Wendel, Ernst Georg. *Studien zur Homiletik Dietrich Bonhoeffers: Predigt, Hermeneutic, Sprache*. Tuebingen: Mohr, 1985.

Wells, Samuel. *God's Companions: Reimagining Christian Ethics*. Oxford: Blackwell, 2006.

———. *Improvisation: The Drama of Christian Ethics*. Grand Rapids: Brazos, 2004.

Wesley, John. "A Farther Appeal to Men of Reason and Religion." In *The Bicentennial Edition of the Works of John Wesley*, vol. 11, edited by Gerald R. Craig. Nashville: Abingdon, 1989.

Williams, A. N. *The Ground of Union: Deification in Aquinas and Palamas*. New York: Oxford University Press, 1999.

Williams, Rowan. *On Christian Theology*. Challenges in Contemporary Theology. Oxford: Blackwell, 2000.

Wirzba, Norman. *The Paradise of God: Renewing Religion in an Ecological Age*. New York: Oxford University Press, 2003.

Wittgenstein, Ludwig. *Philosophical Investigations*. Translated by G. E. M. Anscombe. Oxford: Blackwell, 1997.

Yoder, John Howard. *For the Nations: Essays Public and Evangelical*. Grand Rapids: Eerdmans, 1997.

———. *The Original Revolution: Essays on Christian Pacifism*. Scottdale, PA: Herald, 1998.

———. *The Priestly Kingdom: Social Ethics as Gospel*. Notre Dame, IN: University of Notre Dame Press, 1984.

———. *The Royal Priesthood: Essays Ecclesiological and Ecumenical*. Edited by Michael G. Cartwright. Grand Rapids: Eerdmans, 1994.

Index

Index

Index

in work of Alasdair MacIntyre, 45–50
preaching, 1, 3, 4, 5, 6, 10, 11, 12, 15, 17, 18,
        48, 61, 65, 66–73, 81, 95, 96, 159, 187
    Dietrich Bonhoeffer's theology of,
        82–94
    in early Methodism, 6–7
principalities and powers, 53
    as practices, 53

Radical Orthodoxy, 17, 132, 133, 134,
        142n29, 144, 161
revelation, 139–40
rhetoric, 11, 62, 71, 71n12, 72, 85
Runyan, Theodore, 6

salvation, 5, 8, 10, 42, 85n15, 141, 155, 156,
        186
sanctification, 5, 6, 8, 12, 14, 16, 25, 26, 88,
        165, 187
Schleiermacher, Friedrich, 68–71, 72,
        74n22, 83, 86, 87, 90, 93, 96, 97
Smith, James, 134
Smith, Traci, ix
sociology, 40, 73

Taylor, Barbara Brown, 72
Thomas Aquinas, 104, 112, 113, 114, 115,
        120
Turner, William C. Jr., 12–15, 18

Vatican II, 29, 97–99, 103
von Balthasar, Hans Urs, 41, 43, 177n44

Ward, Graham, 133
Watson, David Lowes, 6
Wells, Samuel, 3, 66, 67
Wesley, Charles, 7–9, 18, 44, 85n60
Wesley, John, 1, 3, 5, 7, 8–10, 12, 14, 16, 186,
        187
Williams, Rowan, 35n42, 36n42, 135,
        159n72
Wittgenstein, Ludwig, 35, 36n42, 37n4,
        67n2, 104, 107, 108
witness, 56, 70, 83, 84, 159, 160, 181, 187
    church's, 41, 91
    practice of, 55

Yoder, John Howard, 53, 59n42, 108n34,
        145n32, 180n50, 184, 187